YES, I CAN — AND — I DID!

The Power of Perseverance

Email: lynda@actiontakerspublishing.com

Website: www.actiontakerspublishing.com

ISBN # (paperback) 978-1-969864-02-5
ISBN # (Kindle) 978-1-969864-03-2
Published by Action Takers Publishing™

Table of Contents

When you say yes, opportunities show themselves. Then it's your choice to take action or not. After all, nothing happens without action. ~Lynda Sunshine West

Introduction

Have you ever been told you're not good enough? Not strong enough? That you're dreaming too big, speaking too loud, or reaching too far?

So have we.

Yes, I Can and I Did! is a powerful collection of stories from 21 individuals who have heard the word **"no"** more times than they can count—but chose to rise anyway. In these pages, you'll meet people who turned rejection into resilience, pain into purpose, and doubt into determination.

These authors come from different backgrounds, cultures, and generations. But they all have one thing in common: at some point, someone (maybe even themselves) told them they couldn't. And instead of shrinking, they stood up. They stepped forward. They said, *Yes, I can. And I did.*

Each chapter is a window into a real-life journey of breakthrough. Some authors overcame adversity in childhood. Others faced fear in adulthood. Many walked away from careers, relationships, or belief systems that no longer served them. All of them chose to rise—again and again.

In this book, you'll hear from:

- **Lynda Sunshine West**, who broke through a lifetime of fear one day at a time.

- **Sally Larkin Green**, who found strength and grace in vulnerability.

- **Alice Pallum**, who reinvented herself after loss and came back stronger.

- **Cathy Derksen**, who dared to walk away from comfort to follow her purpose.

- **Chineme Noke**, who turned injustice into impact by standing in her truth.

- **Christina Thomas**, who used her pain as fuel to empower others.

- *Deremiah *CPE*, who transformed silence and resistance into unstoppable advocacy.

- **Elijah Brassel**, who embraced vulnerability and found freedom through movement.

- **Dr. Erica Buchholz**, who learned that healing doesn't require perfection.

- **Ewa Krempa**, who proved that self-worth isn't given—it's claimed.

- **J.A. Owens**, who found light after darkness and reclaimed her voice.

- **Jacalyn Price**, who rediscovered her identity through creativity and courage.

- **Latara Dragoo**, who chose faith over fear and hope over hiding.

- **Laura Richards**, who stood tall through uncertainty and came out shining.

- **Mary Gould**, who showed that even through grief, joy is possible.

- **Nasirra R Ahamed**, who turned quiet endurance into bold empowerment.

- **Niki Hall**, who let go of shame and stepped into radiant self-love.

- **Pearl Chiarenza**, who used her story to inspire confidence and compassion.

- **Salman Sarwar**, who overcame cultural barriers to live authentically.

- **Sherri Renae Leopold**, who reminds us that standing out is a gift, not a flaw.

- **Tiffiny Jewel Roper**, who turned trauma into triumph and now helps others rise.

This book is a declaration that **you can do hard things**. That your past doesn't define your future. That the things meant to break you can be the very things that build you.

So if you've ever been told *you can't*, let this book whisper back to you:

Yes, you can.

And one day soon, you'll say it too…

Yes, I Can—and I Did.

Lynda Sunshine West and Sally Larkin Green

CHAPTER 1

Do It BECAUSE You're Scared

Lynda Sunshine West

---

*This chapter is dedicated to those who grew up in a
negative environment and want to turn their life around.
I'm here to tell you that you are not destined to repeat
your past. Greatness awaits you. You just have to step
forward and declare, "I can do it. And I will."*

"You're so stupid. You're so ignorant. People are only nice to you because they feel sorry for you."

I heard those words every day for two years. My ex-husband made sure I knew how worthless I was.

But the worst part? He wasn't my worst enemy. *I was.*

I believed every word he said. I repeated them to myself like a twisted lullaby. I told myself I couldn't do anything right, that no one wanted me around, that I was too broken to fix. Unfortunately, his words became my truth—until one day, something inside me cracked open.

It wasn't a lightning bolt moment. It was more like a whisper. A whisper that said, *This isn't who you are.*

But here's the thing about whispers … just like the saying, "When the student is ready, the teacher will appear," you can only hear the whispers when you're finally ready to listen.

Living in Fear's Shadow

Fear was my constant companion. It wasn't just fear of him—it was fear of myself. Fear of what would happen if I left. Fear of what people would think. Fear that maybe, just maybe, he was right about me.

Fear convinced me that staying was safer than leaving. That silence was better than standing up. That surviving was good enough.

But fear lies.

And one day, I got tired of living a life that didn't feel like mine. I didn't know how to leave, but I knew I couldn't keep staying.

So, I did something that terrified me—I left anyway. I literally walked out.

Just me and my two little babies (ages 4 weeks and 14 months), a baby carry case, a diaper bag, a purse. That's it. Nothing more. No car. No plan. No money. No clue what came next. Just a heart pounding so loudly I could hardly hear my own thoughts. But that was the day I unknowingly took the first step toward becoming *me*.

The Year That Changed Everything

Fast forward a few decades later. I was 51 years old and had one of my epiphany moments when I realized that fear was still calling the shots. I had built a safe, predictable life, but deep down, I knew I was still hiding behind old wounds. I was surviving, not thriving.

So, I made a decision that would change everything: I committed to breaking through *one fear every single day for an entire year.*

Three hundred sixty-five fears. One terrified woman. We were on a journey to the unknown.

On Day 1, I was shaking. I made a commitment to ask myself every day for one year, "What scares me?" Then wait until the first fear pops into my head. And, the major commitment, break through THAT fear THAT day no matter how big or small.

Little did I know, those three words would change my life forever. Some days were sort of easy (well, the fears were small). Some days, I cried due to the overwhelming fear I was about to face.

But every day, I showed up scared.

And every day, I broke through the fear that first popped into my head that morning.

That's where the transformation began.

Because courage isn't the absence of fear—it's action *in spite* of it. It's action *BECAUSE* of the fear.

Somewhere along the way, the woman who once believed she was worthless became someone unstoppable. I discovered that fear wasn't my enemy. Fear was my *teacher.*

It showed me what mattered. It revealed my limits and then dared me to go past them. And I did!

Rebuilding the Woman in the Mirror

When you've lived under someone else's control, it takes time to trust yourself again.

I used to think healing meant forgetting the past. But healing is actually remembering without reliving. It's standing in the same storm and realizing you're no longer drowning in it.

Little by little, I rebuilt myself.

I learned that the voice that once called me stupid was never the truth—it was just louder than the real truth. The truth is quieter, kinder, and always there waiting for you to come home to it.

I stopped asking, "Who am I to dream this big?" and started asking, "Who am I *not* to?"

Every time I faced a fear—whether it was public speaking, launching my book publishing business, or simply saying *no*—I was rewriting the narrative of my life.

I didn't just overcome fear. I befriended it.

Now, when fear shows up, I smile and say, "Hey old friend, thanks for reminding me I'm growing again. It's just fear. I must do this *because* I'm scared."

You're Not Broken — You're Becoming

If you're reading this and you're in that place—the place where fear feels louder than your faith—I want you to know something: you are not broken.

You're becoming.

I know what it's like to feel trapped inside your own mind, to replay cruel words until they sound like your own voice. But here's the truth: *they lied.* You are not weak. You are not too late. You are not what they said about you.

Fear will tell you that healing is too hard. That it's safer to stay small. That you don't deserve a fresh start.

But that's exactly why you must do it … because you're scared.

Fear points to the places that need freedom. Every time you move through it, you take back a piece of your power.

My New Definition of Fear

People think fear is a stop sign. It's not. It's a doorway to the possibilities that await you on the other side of the door.

For me, fear now stands for:

Faith

Erases

Anxious

Reactions

It's not something to run from; it's something to run *to* and *through.*

Because on the other side of fear is freedom. On the other side of pain is purpose. And on the other side of "I can't" is the woman who whispers, "Yes, I can, and I did!"

Your Turn

If you're waiting for the fear to go away before you take action, you'll be waiting forever. Courage doesn't come first, action does.

You don't have to be fearless to rebuild your life. You just have to take one small, trembling step forward.

Maybe that step is calling a friend for help. Maybe it's leaving a toxic relationship. Maybe it's finally sharing your story, even if your voice shakes when you tell it.

Whatever it is, I encourage you to do it *because* you're scared. Let your fear fuel you forward.

Because that's how you'll know it matters.

I used to think my scars were reminders of failure. Now I see them as proof that I healed.

I am not who he said I was. I am not who fear tried to convince me to be. I am the woman who broke through 365 fears, left behind the lies, and built a life that once felt impossible.

And if I can do it scared, trembling, and uncertain, *so can you.*

Yes, you can. And you will.

Do it BECAUSE you're scared.

Lynda Sunshine West

Lynda Sunshine West is the Founder of Action Takers Publishing, a woman-owned company helping people worldwide turn their stories into impact. After breaking through one fear a day for an entire year, she discovered her true mission—to inspire others to take action <u>because</u> they're scared, not in spite of it.

A bestselling author, speaker, and show host, Lynda Sunshine empowers entrepreneurs, coaches, and professionals to transform fear into freedom, visibility, and purpose through storytelling and publishing.

Connect with Lynda Sunshine at

<u>https://www.actiontakerspublishing.com</u>

CHAPTER 2

If My Friend Could See Me Now!

Sally Larkin Green

Dedicated to all the Action Takers Authors

It's funny how one comment can change the entire direction of your life. Not because it was inspiring or kind, but because it lit a fire inside you that no one could ever put out.

I still remember the moment like it was yesterday. I had just started dreaming about becoming a coach. I'd been through so many life lessons. I had raised a family, worked in ministry, rediscovered my creativity, and felt this deep pull to help others find their voice and purpose too. I had just written a chapter in my first multi-author collaboration book. I didn't know everything, but I knew enough to know I wanted to make a difference.

Then came the conversation.

A friend of mine, someone I looked up to, stood in front of me one afternoon. She's a college professor, very smart, very confident. I was excited to tell her I was going to attend a talk about marketing your coaching business. I was inspired! My mind was racing with ideas.

But instead of cheering me on, she looked at me with this half-smile and said, "You? A coach? You don't even have a college degree. No one's going to hire you. No one's going to listen to you."

I felt the words hit like a ton of bricks. I tried to explain that I had an associate's degree, that I had just written a chapter in a book, that experience mattered, but she just waved it off. "It's not the same," she said. "Honestly, it's kind of dumb for you to even go to something like that. Coaching and Speaking aren't your thing."

And then she laughed.

That laugh crushed me. It wasn't playful or teasing. It was dismissive. It said, *You're not good enough, and you never will be.*

I smiled politely and changed the subject, but inside, something cracked wide open. That afternoon, I drove home in silence, replaying her words over and over. Every mile I drove, the angrier I got and the hurt grew deeper.

But so did something else.

Somewhere between that broken moment and my front door, I made a promise to myself: *I am going to prove her wrong.*

Not out of anger. Not even to rub it in her face. But because I knew in my heart that she was wrong about me. And I needed to prove it to myself.

So I got to work.

At first, I didn't even know where to start. I began by writing again. I've always loved words. They've been my safe place, my way of healing, and my way of connecting. I joined another collaboration book. I started writing about everything I was learning, all the lessons life had taught me, and before long, those pages turned into stories. Those stories turned into more collaboration books. And those books started changing lives, including my own.

Then came the speaking. Oh, how terrifying that was at first! I still laugh when I think about my first time going live on Zoom. My hands were shaking, my voice was quivering, and I remember thinking, *Well, this might be the worst idea I've ever had.* But my friend Lynda gave me the gentle push I needed, and I did it anyway. And guess what? People listened. Not because I had a fancy degree hanging on the wall, but because I spoke from the heart.

That's when I realized something powerful. People don't connect with your credentials. They connect with your authenticity.

Over the last four years, I've built a career I once only dreamed about. I've spoken at events, led workshops, written and published books, and helped others become bestselling authors. I've coached writers through their fears, helped them find their voice, and watched them step into their own power. Every time I get to do that, I think back to that conversation and smile.

Not in spite, but in gratitude.

Because if she hadn't doubted me, maybe I wouldn't have pushed this hard. Maybe I would have stayed comfortable, believing I wasn't qualified enough to follow my calling. Sometimes God uses the very people who doubt us to propel us into our purpose.

There have been times along the way when her words echoed back, whispering, *You're not good enough.* When I faced rejection or a project didn't go as planned, I'd hear that laugh again in the back of my mind. But instead of letting it stop me, I let it fuel me. It reminded me that I had something to prove. Not to her, but to myself and to the God who put this dream in my heart.

Today, I stand on stages, coach authors, and write books that reach readers all over the world. And I do it all without needing anyone's permission. It was never my lack of a proper degree holding me back. It was my confidence that needed to grow. Once I stopped viewing myself through someone else's limitations and started believing in my own potential, everything began to open up.

That doesn't mean I never struggle. I still have moments of doubt, and that little voice of imposter syndrome still tries to sneak in sometimes. But now I recognize it for what it is—fear dressed up as logic. I've learned to thank it for showing up and move forward anyway.

The truth is, your worth isn't determined by a title or a piece of paper. It's measured by the lives you touch, the courage you show, and the faith you hold when others don't believe in you.

Now, when I look back on that conversation, I actually smile. Because if my "friend" could see me now, standing in front of audiences, publishing books, helping others chase their dreams, she'd probably be surprised. But honestly? I'm not. Because I always knew there was something more inside me waiting to shine.

It just took someone's disbelief to bring it out.

I learned something beautiful through all of this. When someone tells you "you can't," they're really showing you the limits of their imagination, not yours. Don't ever let someone else's fear or pride define what's possible for your life. You get to decide that.

So to anyone who's ever been told they're not smart enough, not qualified enough, not the "type," hear me when I say this: you already have what it takes. You don't need permission to walk in your purpose. You just need the courage to start.

If my friends could see me now, they'd see a woman who stopped waiting for approval and created her own path. They'd see someone who turned pain into purpose, doubt into determination, and a hurtful comment into a mission to help others rise.

They'd see that the best degree I ever earned wasn't from a college. It was from the school of life, faith, and persistence. And let me tell you, the graduation ceremony has been incredible.

Sally Larkin Green

Sally Larkin Green is a bestselling author, speaker, and book coach who helps writers turn their stories into messages that inspire and transform. As President of Action Takers Publishing, she has guided hundreds of authors from idea to publication, helping them share their voices with confidence and purpose.

After years of teaching Sunday school and serving in ministry, Sally discovered that storytelling was her true calling. Her own journey, marked by faith, resilience, and a determination to rise above doubt, has shaped the foundation of her work today. She now speaks at events, leads writing workshops, and creates spaces where people can heal, grow, and shine through the power of words.

Sally is also the author of children's books and faith-based studies that encourage readers to live with joy, courage, and authenticity. Whether she's leading a Bible study, coaching a first-time author, or writing her next book, her heart's mission remains the same: to help others see what's possible when they say, "Yes I can."

Connect with Sally, explore her books, or learn how to work with her at <u>FindSally.com</u>.

CHAPTER 3

Resilience in Action

Alice Pallum

Resilience becomes real when life gives you moments you never expected. To me, it wasn't about simply "bouncing back." It was about moving forward when the road looked nothing like the one I had planned. It was the choice to reinvent, to rebuild, and to rise— again and again.

My story isn't one of smooth sailing. It's a story of setbacks that forced me to grow in ways I never imagined. From losing a corporate job I thought was secure, to facing a health crisis that changed my life, to navigating a global pandemic that threatened my business, I had plenty of chances to give up. Each time, I chose to dig in and move forward. This is my journey of resilience, proof that no matter what comes our way, we can say: *Yes, I can, and I did.*

The Unexpected Turn—Losing My Job at American Express

For 17 years, I built my career at American Express, beginning at IDS Financial Services before it was purchased by the company. It felt like a steady foundation. I had a role I understood, colleagues I respected, and confidence in my abilities. I thought I found my lane for the long haul.

Then, almost without warning, it was gone. My position was eliminated.

The news hit me hard. I had been a strong performer with excellent reviews and awards. Suddenly, the stability I counted on was gone. The question that echoed in my head was, *"What do I want to do when I grow up this time?"*

The first decision was clear: I would not work for someone else again. After 17 years building expertise, I didn't want my future to be controlled by someone else's chart. I decided to start my own business.

I began with consulting, guided by my background in technology. The early weeks were filled with uncertainty—how to structure the business, who to contact, what to charge. There was fear, but also excitement. I realized that while the job had been taken from me, my skills, creativity, and determination were my own.

Starting a business without a roadmap is messy. I made mistakes, took on projects that didn't fit, and learned quickly how to say no. Each misstep taught me a lesson about resilience: persistence and adaptability keep you moving forward. Losing my job became a strange blessing. It pushed me into entrepreneurship and into discovering strengths I hadn't yet met.

Rebuilding After My Stroke

Eight years into building my business, life threw another curveball—I had a stroke.

Everything I had worked so hard to build felt like it was slipping through my fingers. The stroke affected me physically, mentally, and emotionally. It took nine months to recover enough to move back into my own home. Simple tasks were difficult; the energy I once relied on to fuel my business vanished overnight.

Resilience isn't always bold or dramatic. Sometimes it shows up as a quiet, stubborn decision to do the next small thing. That's what rebuilding looked like—slow, steady progress: one step, one sentence, one small victory at a time.

I had to relearn reading, writing, walking. I had to accept that some things I once did easily now took more time. I adjusted expectations, gave myself grace, and preserved my energy for the most important parts of my business. Over time, I realized resilience isn't about returning to who you were; it's about becoming who you are meant to be. My stroke forced me to slow down while giving me clarity. I learned that progress matters more than perfection.

Pivoting During COVID

Just as I found my rhythm again, life threw another curveball: COVID.

Overnight, the world shut down. Workshops, in-person events, and connections that fueled my business disappeared. It wasn't just a logistical challenge; it required a whole new way of thinking.

Resilience doesn't mean you never feel afraid. It means you keep showing up anyway.

I adapted. I moved my coaching and consulting work online, learned new tools, and reimagined how to reach and support people virtually. I missed the energy of a room full of business owners sharing ideas, but slowly, something shifted. This pivot opened new doors. I connected with clients beyond my area and even spoke internationally. My work became more flexible, creative, and impactful. COVID taught me resilience is often built through a series of pivots: willingness to try, willingness to fail, and the grit to try again.

Now—Building New Courses and Evergreen Items

Today I am in a season of growth by choice. After so many unexpected turns, I've learned that change doesn't have to be feared; it can be created.

I'm focused on building new courses and evergreen programs. I'm creating resources that let me help more people, in more places, without being limited by time or location. This work feels like the natural next step. It brings together everything I've learned through each challenge: how to simplify, serve, and keep moving forward.

This time, I'm building with intention. My focus isn't growth for growth's sake; it's about creating something sustainable, meaningful, and impactful—something that continues to help others even when I'm not in the room.

Through loss, recovery, reinvention, and renewal, resilience has shaped every chapter of my story. It isn't a single moment of strength. It's a mindset: a quiet, steady belief that no matter what happens, you can rise, rebuild, and begin again. If I could do it, so can you.

Alice Pallum

Alice Pallum helps business owners and entrepreneurs turn complexity into clarity and action. As a strategist and consultant, she guides clients in making informed decisions and achieving measurable results—even when the path forward feels uncertain.

As the founder of AMP Business Coaching and Consulting—Where Strategy and Accountability Meet—Alice works with business owners to identify priorities, set meaningful goals, and implement strategies that move their businesses forward. Her approach combines practical planning and structured accountability to ensure clients achieve sustainable progress.

Through workshops, courses, and one-on-one consulting, Alice helps entrepreneurs break down challenges, streamline processes, and align daily operations with long-term objectives. She believes lasting success comes from combining effective systems with disciplined execution, enabling business owners to operate efficiently while staying focused on growth.

Alice's mission is to help entrepreneurs build businesses that work for them—businesses where they can serve clients, innovate, and scale with confidence. She provides the tools, frameworks, and actionable guidance that frees business owners to focus on their expertise while knowing they have structured support every step of the way.

With Alice's guidance, business owners move from uncertainty to clarity, from ideas to action, and from strategy to tangible results— building businesses that reflect their purpose, passion, and potential.

Connect with Alice at http://ampbusinesscoaching.com

CHAPTER 4

Inspiration and Tenacity Lead the Way to Success

Cathy Derksen

I dedicate this chapter to women around the world who are taking on new challenges in life.

If you had asked me five years ago what I would be doing at this point in my life, the answer would not have come close to describing my current reality. There was nothing in my past careers or life experience that even hinted about the path that would lead me here.

Fifteen years ago, a message came to me intuitively. It was simply a thought with no image or details. The message told me that I was going to develop a career doing something that created a true impact in the lives of women around the world. That was the whole message.

I wasn't given any hints about what that would look like or how to get there. It took me over a decade to find my way, but I made it!

A Wake-Up Call That Changed Everything

Back in 2008, I was living in a toxic, abusive marriage and working in a very negative setting that was challenging my wellbeing in both my mental and physical health. It took the shock and trauma of a fatal car accident to wake me up to the undesirable way I had been living my life. This event set me on a new course to rediscover my passion and create a life that brought me joy and inspiration. I had no idea how I was going to take my life in a new direction, but I had a deep trust in myself that I could figure it out. At the age of 47, I set out to find my true calling.

It was in those days of sorting through my life that I received my intuitive message about creating true impact in the lives of women around the world. What did it mean? Which direction should I go? I had no idea, so I started taking the next best step forward. I began working on personal development and joining communities of inspiring, supportive people. Step by step I moved forward.

In the middle of this self-discovery and career transformation, I left my abusive marriage and took on the role of a single mom supporting my two teenagers through the turmoil of our shifting family dynamics. It was a challenging time for all of us. I knew we were on the right path but getting over some of the hurdles required a solid focus on survival.

Based on my previous life experience, I looked at traditional careers that might allow me to have a positive impact in women's lives. I decided to shift my career into financial planning thinking this could be the answer. I jumped in with everything I had, completing my full Certified Financial Planner credentials as well as my insurances licences. I worked with dozens of women and supported their financial journey with tools and resources, but I felt this was not the true impact I was here to make. After a decade of working as a financial planner, I came to the decision that this was not the path I was meant to follow if I was going to develop my full potential. At the age of 57, I made the massive decision to become an entrepreneur so I could create the career that fit my dreams.

Finding My True Calling

In 2019 was the first time I felt a calling to share my story in a published book. Before that, I hadn't felt the need to write a book or get involved in the publishing industry. It was nowhere on the life path I had seen for myself before. A local group of women had been putting together collaborative books for a few years. I had been aware of them but hadn't felt any need to participate. It wasn't until the book titled, *Emotional Intelligence: Mental Health Matter* was announced that I felt a need to share my story. I experienced what I describe as a calling. There was a force inside of me insisting that my story needed to be in that book so it could help other women experiencing similar life challenges. This was the beginning of my journey on the path that would lead me to fulfilling my life mission.

It's been six years since I submitted my chapter in that first book. I discovered I loved the process of putting my story on paper and releasing it out into the world. I loved the community that was created in the team of authors in the book, and I was surprised by the doors that opened as I embraced the world of publishing. To date, I have contributed to over 20 anthologies. Each one is focused on a different theme and includes a different community of inspiring people.

Creating Global Impact Through Storytelling

As I was working on my sixth book, I recognized my passion for sharing stories in my community of women. I realized this was the answer to the intuitive message I had received years ago. This is how I can create a true impact in the lives of women around the world. I now focus my passion on bringing together women from every corner of the globe to share their stories in multi-author books similar to this one. My books have titles and themes that women are inspired to write about and read about. As women, we gain a lot of value through sharing our stories. We inspire and motivate each other to take on new challenges. We learn that we are not alone in the journey we call life. I am honored to have worked with over 200 women, giving them the opportunity to share their stories and become published authors.

When I first set out to transform my negative family life and career into my life passion, I had no idea where I was going. It was through following my intuition, connecting with my inspirations, and applying tenacity to overcome the challenges, that I have been able to create this life I love.

Cathy Derksen

Cathy Derksen is the passionate founder of Inspired Tenacity, an international speaker, publisher, and 20x #1 bestselling author. After reimagining her own life in her 50s, Cathy discovered her mission: to help midlife women embrace new possibilities and boldly share their stories. She believes that authorship and community are the keys to true impact—both for the storyteller and the lives they touch.

Through her multi-author book projects, retreats, and vibrant community, Cathy has helped over 200 women become published authors, amplifying their visibility, expanding their businesses, and building lasting legacies. Her programs are more than platforms— they're launching pads for purpose-driven transformation.

Cathy lives by the mantra, "Do what makes you come alive," and brings that energy into everything she creates. When she's not mentoring women to stand in their power, you'll find her recharging in nature, soaking in the inspiration around her.

Explore her work at www.inspiredtenacity.com.

CHAPTER 5

Me v. The Government Legal Service and Civil Service Commissioners (GLS)

Chineme Noke

---

*To my daughter Amadi, the brightest light of my life, who
taught me that life is for living and not just for working;
and to my dear, departed father, my absolute hero, who
taught me that self-belief and persistence are the keys to
success and happiness.*

The court's landmark decision was published during the summer of 1996.

In 1990, as a trainee attorney, I was made a manager of a team of lawyers, before I had formally qualified, in my first job after graduation. I left that organization after two years as a fully-fledged corporate lawyer, and went into freelance consultancy work for another two years in order to experience various other legal corporations within the public and private sectors.

I was then encouraged to apply for a senior position within the Treasury Solicitor's Department of the UK GLS, which was said to be an elite group of top-notch lawyers, all of whom had been through an onerous recruitment process.

Once shortlisted and invited for an interview, I attended and was presented with an hour-long written examination which I completed in less than 30 minutes. I therefore used the remaining time to neatly rewrite all of my original answers, folded up my original papers, and placed them in my purse, despite instructions to the contrary. After all, the answers were my own.

At my appointed time, I was led into the interview room where the seated panel consisted of three elderly, white males who appeared to be totally astonished at my presence! As a tall, Black woman, I had become accustomed to being gaped at as though I must surely have taken a wrong turn. I gave them my brightest greetings as I duly took the seat facing them.

The interview began with the Chief Treasury Solicitor introducing himself and his colleagues, prior to me answering their introductory questions about my early life, educational background, qualifications and work history. Not once did the Treasury Solicitor crack a smile throughout the entire process, although his wingmen seemed more amenable to polite exchanges.

At one point during the interview, one of my answers elicited the cry of, "That's genius!" by the one to my right, which was met with an angry glare from the Chief. They later hotly refuted this "contretemps"! I smiled politely and remained composed.

After an hour, the interview was complete; I knew I'd done very well and rose to leave. The one on my right stood, smiled, and shook my hand before walking me to the door. The other two did not.

Feeling extremely confident of my knowledge, performance and general interaction, I virtually skipped myself out of the building, smiling all the way home.

A few days later, the letter arrived and I tore open the envelope excitedly, scanning it quickly for the expected good news. My eyes went straight to the second paragraph which began, "Unfortunately... and so you will not be proceeding to the next stage."

Although disappointed, I called Human Resources and requested some written feedback, expecting the usual, "The quality of candidates was very high, the decision was difficult..." However, the letter stated that I had "performed below the required standard and was clearly out of my depth." I felt as though I had been sucker-punched and had to sit down before my legs collapsed beneath me.

Silent tears ran down my face. I stared into the distance and my disbelief slowly turned into abject anger. How dare they treat me like this?! I certainly was not going to go away quietly; they were not going to get away with this injustice! I knew my worth, as did the many previous organisations for which I had worked and consulted.

As the days passed, my resolve grew stronger. I had no option but to begin court proceedings against this organisation which was the highest recruiter of lawyers in the country. I was certain that I had right on my side, and I would use the justice system within which we all operated to prove it.

My only surprise was the reaction of the people around me; both friends and family tried their best to talk me out of my decided course of action. I received cries of, "You simply cannot win against this huge, governmental entity!" and, "You will be silenced, one way or another!" Yes, really.

At every turn I faced nervous, fearful objections to my intended plan of action. My response was, "Yes, I can, and I WILL!" I was fed up with the constant inequality caused by the blatant race and sex discrimination; the misogyny and misogynoir that the majority of us were subjected to - and with which we were expected to endure, without complaint.

I was a relatively young attorney without the resources to single-handedly take on this huge behemoth of an organisation that enjoyed unlimited resources. Nevertheless, I began preparing for my legal challenge by requesting redacted copies of the applications of, and comments on, the hundreds of shortlisted candidates, and meticulously scrutinized them over many days and nights, noting the glaring differences between the treatment of male and female, then black/brown and white candidates.

It was glaringly obvious to me that there was both race and sex discrimination being routinely practiced on an alarming scale. Armed with this indisputable evidence, I sought backing from the National Equalities Commission, given the widespread effects of the flawed decision-making on the general public.

I was accepted and allocated a similarly recently qualified Barrister (Trial Counsel) who just happened to be a young, white lady alongside whom I had studied as an undergraduate for our Law Degrees, with Honors! The coincidence (or not) was unreal.

After much reminiscing and laughter, we got down to business with the legal preparations for my seminal court case, ensuring that no stone was left unturned.

The preparatory work took many months, after which the hearing date was set. However, the other side did not appear, citing the requirement of the Chief Treasury Lawyer at a military trial in Cyprus!

The hearing was relisted with a stern warning from the court that there would be serious consequences should they again fail to appear.

When we eventually made it to trial, the GLS was late. We waited inside the courtroom until the doors were theatrically flung open, revealing a long line of men in black, trailed by a woman who announced herself as the GLS's stenographer.

The proceedings began with my Counsel outlining my case, followed by their Counsel outlining their defence, which was basically that I was rubbish in all aspects.

I then explained my position in full, as did they, including my "poor" performances in both the written test and the interview. Of course, our accounts were diametrically opposed.

The next day, cross examinations continued, with more of the same untruths from them.

The judges requested copies of the written examination, their model answers, and the redacted applications, which they smirkingly handed over.

The judges then asked whether I had anything to add, to which my Counsel proffered the first copy of my written answers to assist with their deliberations.

The Chief Treasury Lawyer leapt to his feet shouting, "Nothing was meant to be removed!" and insisting that I must have created it later.

However, having seen it, they had to admit that the document was indeed GLS paper which could not have been obtained elsewhere.

The court adjourned for the judges to consider all the evidence, and set a hearing for their final decision.

A few weeks later, we all returned. The other side were visibly uncomfortable as we all took our seats within the packed courtroom. The buzz was silenced as the panel was seated. The lead judge glanced around the room before getting right into it.

"This is a claim by CN of race and sex discrimination throughout an extensive recruitment process by the GLS..."

It seemed like forever as the minutes ticked by until eventually, she stated, "This court unanimously finds for the Claimant..."

I had done it! I defeated the GLS and they were ordered to pay me extensive damages, as well as create Equalities Policies and Procedures with appropriate training for all of their personnel to prevent such inequalities from recurring.

I was able to victoriously say, "Yes I can, and I DID!" And so can YOU!

Chineme Noke

A Corporate Lawyer who spent over 20 years leading teams of law-yers and other professionals, Chineme studied for many post-graduate diplomas, including an MBA with the Open University, had Director-ships at Lawyers in Local Government Ltd and Special Hidden Tal-ents Ltd, and was a member of the Chartered Institute of Managers.

Chineme is now an internet entrepreneur, success coach, speaker and author who believes that success is not just about the finances; more importantly, it is about taking responsibility for our own future, right now.

Chineme helps people to overcome the very real problems they face which can overwhelm and rob them of their well-being and happiness. She does this by dealing effectively with what she refers to as the mountains and molehills that we all encounter in our daily lives.

In one of her published works, *"There Is No Time Like the Present to Create Your Future,"* Chineme formulated seven action steps in order that anybody can take charge of their present to create for themselves a better future. They are action steps that will change attitudes and, indeed, people's lives.

Her memoir, "*Special Hidden Talents: One Mother's Personal Journey Through the World of Special Education Needs*," and her many other anthologies, are available on Amazon.

Join Chineme's community, *Female Empowerment, Women Entrepreneurs: Unstoppable Shepreneurs*, at

https://www.unstoppableshepreneurs.group/.

CHAPTER 6

Yes I Can Lose Weight and Keep It Off!

Christina Thomas

---

*To my family & dog, Thanks for being sweeter
than stevia!*

Today I'm so grateful that I can eat whatever I want most days without worrying about gaining weight.

It wasn't always this way... Both sides of my family tree are adorned with extra pounds, and I assumed I was doomed to follow in their heavy footsteps. Growing up, I watched my mother try Weight Watchers and a host of other diet and exercise programs. So when I needed to lose weight, I tried the same "solutions." My ADHD and its associated motivational challenges combined with impulsivity, disorganization, and a lack of focus and time management skills made it particularly difficult to stick with weight loss programs. Like most people, after losing a few pounds, I'd end up "finding" more than I lost—which made me even more frustrated with myself.

Sometimes breakthroughs come from unusual sources. My weight loss breakthrough came from breaking actual bones! Trying to relive my competitive figure-skating glory days nearly two decades later, an off-kilter jump resulted in a shattered ankle. All of a sudden, activities I previously took for granted (exercising, showering, and climbing up two flights of stairs to my condo) were much more difficult.

After installing a metal plate and nine screws in my ankle, a very painful surgery, my orthopedic surgeon said I'd need to be off my feet for several weeks, and then should be able to resume normal activity after 12 weeks of physical therapy. I told him "normal activity" for me that time of year meant snowboarding. A skier himself, he understood. He said if my recovery went smoothly, it *might* be possible.

The injury couldn't have come at a worse time—just weeks before I was scheduled to fly to Japan for a bucket-list snowboarding and sightseeing trip I had booked a year in advance. Thankfully, travel insurance provided a refund for my cancelled trip, but I couldn't get my multi-resort annual ski pass refunded. Adding insult to literal injury was the fact that it was the final season that a single pass would provide access to both Whistler Blackcomb in Canada, and my home ski resort in California, Mammoth Mtn. While my then-boyfriend (now ex-husband) and friends enjoyed an epic ski season with record snowfall, I desperately wanted in on the action! So I did something radical: I booked a ski trip to Whistler for week 13 of my recovery. Snow FOMO became a powerful external motivator!

My physical therapist—who had treated me for previous issues— knew my less-than-stellar track record w/ doing my PT exercises at home. When I told her I needed my ankle to be ready to snowboard by week 13, she said she wasn't sure if it would be possible—despite the surgeon's statement. I told her I already had a Plan B for the trip: If I couldn't actually snowboard by then, I'd spend my days at the nearby hot springs spa.

But the upcoming ski trip turned out to be just the motivation I needed to not only do my PT exercises regularly but also lose some weight to help speed my recovery. My shattered ankle also provided a very practical reason to lose weight: The American College of Foot & Ankle Surgeons says that each extra pound of body weight can put up to eight pounds of extra pressure on our ankles with each step, and that losing even a few pounds can significantly reduce pressure on our ankles.

Determined to be riding the slopes of Whistler on week 13, I made time for my PT exercises. At the same time, I developed a flexible, ADHD-friendly science-based weight management system that has served me throughout the years, keeping me feeling young and energetic! I've been able to maintain the weight loss, and knowing that I can easily control my weight is truly a comfort.

I was thrilled beyond belief when (much to my physical therapist's pleasant surprise) I was able to snowboard on week 13. I'll never forget that first run. After exiting the chair lift, I couldn't believe how normal everything felt! And it only got better. After riding through a lovely glade of trees, when I popped back out onto the slope, I experienced "snowshine" (when it starts snowing while still sunny) for the first time. It felt as if Ullr, the Norse god of snow and skiing, was celebrating with me!

While I would never choose to get injured, I'm glad this experience had a silver lining! These days, I enjoy teaching fellow adults with ADHD—as well as tour managers who work on the road—how to achieve similar results.

Some things in life are beyond our control. I love teaching people how weight doesn't have to be one of them!

Christina Thomas

Christina Thomas is a tour director, weight loss coach, and the founder of Wanderlust Weight Loss, an innovative science-backed weight management program catering to adults with ADHD and tour directors. As a member of the International Association of Positive Psychology Coaches, a hobbyist standup comic, and volunteer adaptive ski and snowboard instructor with Disabled Sports Eastern Sierra/Access Mammoth, Christina loves mentoring and teaching through humor.

A former CBS TV news reporter and producer, she pioneered her way into media technology sales as the first female salesperson hired by Chyron in 35 years, before serving as VP of Sales for media tech startup Stringr Inc.

Connect with Christina at https://wanderlustweightloss.com

CHAPTER 7
Silenced in Arizona

Deremiah *CPE

I'd like to Dedicate this Chapter to all the great women and men who've devoted their entire lives in service to the United State Army, Marines, Air Force, Navy, Coast Guard, and National Guard. Including every First Responder who shows up ready to lay down their lives helping others.

---

138 letters. Nine months. Zero justice.

Picture this: You do everything right. You write the letters. File the complaints. Name names. Cite the laws. You place the truth into the hands of people sworn to uphold it. Blackmail. Misconduct. Denial of due process. The kind of material that should trigger investigations—or headlines.

Instead, you get silence. Or worse—robotic responses designed to sound official but say nothing at all.

This wasn't theoretical. It happened. And I lived it.

There was a time for over 30 years that I stood on local and national stages as an honored child advocate. Now, I stand in the margins—not because I failed, but because I refused to be silent. What I lost wasn't my home. It was the illusion that justice is automatic.

This isn't just a story about being unhoused. It's the anatomy of a system that counts on you not being heard.

In August 2024, I began documenting misconduct in Arizona's law enforcement and political offices. What started as a single report evolved into a wall of silence—an institutional refusal to engage.

By April 2025, I sent over 138 formal letters, and copied 263 others—journalists, legal groups, oversight bodies. Most went unanswered. A few came back with vague boilerplate replies. The rest disappeared into the void.

But silence is a signal. And I followed it.

Every email they ignored. Every question they dodged. And every deflected public record request became data. I built timelines. Tracked responses. Logged patterns. What they didn't say became my evidence.

This isn't a chapter about survival; it's a blueprint for anyone forced to confront the lies without resources.

They said this couldn't be done.

I documented the proof that it was.

Arizona's failure to respond wasn't a glitch. It was design. Silence wasn't random. It was tactical. When a homeless man sends official letters, they expect them to vanish without consequence.

But silence can be measured. It can be tracked. And I did just that.

One letter documented blackmail…the other the silence of law enforcement. Another requested bodycam footage under Arizona's public records law: A.R.S. §39-121. I filed them all properly. Repeatedly. Still—no investigation. No audit. No response beyond polite brush-offs.

So I built the ledger. I recorded all interactions. Each omission. Every non-answer.

The hardest part wasn't being ignored. It was staying focused while homeless—piecing together a forensic archive on borrowed Wi-Fi and shared devices. There were no whiteboards or boardrooms—just notebooks, email timestamps, and the clarity of having nothing left to lose.

I didn't ask for justice. I assembled its absence.

Now I'm using that work to press forward—into legal action, public visibility, and a TEDx stage designed to make this story unignorable.

This isn't about vengeance. It's about making suppression visible. Because when silence becomes state policy, someone has to name it.

They told me I wouldn't survive this.

Yet here you are, reading my words.

If you've ever been dismissed, disregarded, or erased—know this: your silence isn't empty. It's recordable. And if you document enough of it, eventually it becomes the loudest voice in the room.

You don't need millions of followers to speak your truth. You just need documentation, endurance, and a fire that can't be put out—even by a system designed to ignore you.

If this story hits home, don't scroll past it. If it stirs something in you, follow it. Because it's only reminding you of a time you weren't being heard.

Silence has always been the final defense of the powerful.

And now?

"Silenced In Arizona" has a name.

And it won't go unheard. Because I did what they said you can't do and so can you.

Deremiah *CPE

Deremiah *CPE doesn't just show up—he shifts entire conversations.

An international award-winning inspirational speaker, legacy educator, and marketing strategist, Deremiah has built a reputation for delivering real solutions where others offer empty noise. He's been named one of MarketingProfs' Top 25 Experts Worldwide, and has electrified audiences across platforms like CBS Radio, Sirius XM, and Cumulus Media with his message of grit, growth, and grassroots impact.

But what sets him apart isn't just voice. It's evidence.

As the first-ever Hometown HERO-Educator, Deremiah received the American Red Cross' highest civilian community service award. His humanitarian work earned him the prestigious Nightingale Conant Lifetime Achievement Award—recognizing decades of advocacy for vulnerable children and underserved communities.

Now, with Silenced In Arizona, he breaks new ground: confronting political suppression and systemic silence head-on. With 138 formal complaints filed, Deremiah turned state-level suppression into a forensic campaign for truth and transparency.

He's not looking for pity. He's writing the playbook for public resistance.

Truth has a new address.

And it's signed—Deremiah *CPE

Connect with Deremiah at https://talks.co/deremiahcpe.

CHAPTER 8

Rise Above It: The Undeniable Power of Believing in Yourself

Elijah Brassel

I dedicate this chapter to my wonderful late mother, Lashanda Brassel, who passed away in July 2024. Without her, I wouldn't be the man I am today. Her unconditional love and support have been my pillar of strength and my biggest motivation for achieving greater success.

Ever since I was a child, I've always had a deep infatuation with music and dancing. It lights up my soul, spirit, and imagination. There came a time in my life when I questioned whether I was meant to dance at all—not because my love for it withered away, but because the people in my circle doubted my capability, and that caused me to feel like I wasn't good enough to be considered a dancer.

Dancing wasn't just a hobby to me; it was something I was truly passionate about. I've always gravitated towards it and danced with all of my heart in every session. I had a burning desire to move and improve, and poured everything I had into it but, despite the massive amount of dedication I possessed, I rarely received positive feedback from those around me. Instead, I was met with doubt and sometimes even ridicule.

Friends who I had known for years weren't very supportive of my dancing; sometimes they'd cringe, twist their face, and even just flat out ignore me altogether.

Me and my friends used to ride around in a pickup truck. One time when we were hanging out in the back of the truck, we were parked next to a bar that had an outside dining area full of people. The atmosphere was very lively and the establishment played all sorts of catchy tunes. So, naturally, I wanted to get up and groove right then and there. I expressed my desire to dance to my friends and two of them told me not to do it because I'd just embarrass myself. I expressed to them how hurtful their comments were to me and suddenly I was met with pity. They proceeded to say things like, "You're the best dancer in the world," "You're extremely talented at dancing," "Everyone thinks you're great at dancing," so on and so forth. I felt completely discouraged, like no matter how passionate I was I would never be good enough for anyone to believe in me and decided not to dance.

One of the harshest blows I've ever received came from my first ex-girlfriend. On one hot, sunny day in June, me and my friend went on a double date with my ex and her friend at a community pool. After some time of swimming and conversing with each other, I just had a random urge to dance, so that's exactly what I did. I hopped out of the water and danced joyfully like no one was watching.

After the date ended, I was stuck on Cloud 9 the entire car ride home, but my high abruptly came crashing down. Later that day, my ex sent me a text that made my heart drop deep into my gut. Her exact words to me were, "You're not good at dancing at all. You completely embarrassed me so don't dance around me in public ever again." Those words stung painfully deep inside my heart and tormented my mind a lot longer than I'd like to admit. I began to question not only my talent, but my right to express myself at all.

Despite the shame I felt from her judgment and all those who've doubted me, my passion for dancing never went away. That pain became unlimited fuel for me. It caused me to develop a chip on my shoulder every time I moved. I had enough of being counted out, so I made a promise to myself that I would silence their doubt and prove to myself that I am capable of becoming a phenomenal dancer. That's when my dancing took its first steps.

In 2017, at 19 years old, I auditioned for the most well-known and respected dance organization at Northern Illinois University and made the team. Every member was extremely skilled and passionate with a lifetime of dance experience. They inspired me daily to grow beyond my current skill level, and it paid off tremendously. We performed at many shows and events together, constantly pushing the boundaries of what we called dance.

In the year and a half that I've spent with them, my dance talent improved at an exponentially significant rate! Over time, I built a solid foundation to cultivate my own unique style. I became so good at dancing that crowds cheered for me in amazement from my moves—something I've yearned to experience for so long.

Eventually, I left the dance organization and joined forces with another ex-member from the NIU dance team. We formed our own team named "2Krucial Squad" and that brought about the opportunity of a lifetime.

In 2018, I performed on *World of Dance* at just 20 years old with my teammates! It felt like stepping into another realm of existence— one where dance was the universal language. The energy, the freestyle sessions, the crowds—it was electrifying! I could only describe it as "Dance Heaven." That experience single handedly solidified my confidence in myself as a dancer and left me feeling 100% certain of myself. I was born to dance.

A year later, my life shifted tremendously.

In 2019, I posted a photo on Instagram that unexpectedly went viral overnight. I woke up to 5,000 likes which quickly soared to over 10,000 likes the next day. Suddenly I had everyone's attention, and my dance videos began gaining an insane amount of traction. I created a shuffling tutorial that received 273,000 views and 26,000 likes on TikTok in the span of a week.

I then came up with an idea to showcase dance moves into a 5-part series from the '90s era which turned out to be a complete success:

- Part 1: 41,000 views
- Part 2: 594,000 views
- Part 3: 297,000 views
- Part 4: 49,000 views
- Part 5: 20,400 views

My viral success continued from a tutorial I posted to TikTok on how to do the arm wave and to this day it still holds the record for my most viewed dance video of all time with over 800,000 views and over 69,000 likes. In 2025, another dance video I posted on my TikTok page went viral again—I was dancing at a yacht party in Miami having the time of my life and that video blew UP like crazy receiving 650,000 views and 72,000 likes, making it my most liked dance video to date.

The exposure I gained throughout the years has attracted many Brand sponsorships starting with **The Coldest Water** (395K TikTok followers, 105K on Instagram) back in 2020, which was a major milestone for me. Since then, I've collaborated with the following brands:

- **Duradry** (15.8K IG followers)
- **Himistry** (62.2K IG followers)
- **Bumpboxx** (322K IG followers)
- **Glow Beverages/DrinkGlow** (194K IG Followers) [Sponsored by Kylie Jenner]
- **Wavenforcer** (5K IG followers)
- **Firstline Brands** (13.7K IG followers)

Every collaboration represented a step forward—not just in reach, but in personal validation. I was no longer focused on proving something to others; I was simply becoming someone I could be proud of.

As a result of the past six years spent as a content creator/influencer, I now have 95,000 followers on TikTok with 5 million likes in total and counting, 60,000 followers on Instagram, 25,000 followers on threads, and 2,000 subscribers on YouTube.

Looking back, I've come to realize something extremely powerful: the doubts of others may have ignited the fire but truly it was passion, discipline, and my love for the craft that kept the flames burning. I am no longer dancing to prove them wrong; I dance because it's just what I love doing more than anything in life.

"I am no longer fueled by doubt—I am driven by purpose, passion, and the undeniable power of believing in myself." ~Elijah Brassel

---

Elijah Brassel

Elijah Brassel is a dynamic influencer and content creator who has built a powerful online presence rooted in authenticity, resilience, and purpose. With over 190,000 followers across all social media platforms and more than 5 million likes to his name, Elijah has cultivated a thriving digital community by staying true to his vision—even when others doubted him.

A passionate storyteller and motivator, Elijah uses his platforms not just to entertain, but to empower others to silence self-doubt and rise above negativity. His journey hasn't always been easy, but it's that very adversity that fuels his message: you can overcome anything when you refuse to let outside voices define your worth.

Featured in this book as a voice of determination and belief, Elijah brings a firsthand perspective on what it takes to keep showing up for yourself—even when the world tells you not to. His work continues to inspire the next generation of creators, dreamers, and doers to stand tall in their truth and move forward with confidence.

Elijah's story is a testament to the power of faith, focus, and fearlessness—and a reminder that the greatest success often begins in the face of the strongest doubt.

Connect with Elijah at https://linktr.ee/Elijah18.

CHAPTER 9

Diapers, Dirt, and Doubt: Why Taking My 6-Month-Old Camping Was a Parenting Masterclass

Dr. Erica Buchholz

To the weary parents who shared their truth with me. Your honesty fuels my work. Thank you for opening up your lives so I can champion you and your amazing children, whose light and joy make every single day worth it.

"There is no way you can take a baby camping. He's too little! What if he cries in the middle of the night? What are you going to do with the diapers? What if there are ticks?"

Phew!

Being a parent can be tough; am I right?

There are so many voices telling us what is right, what is wrong, the better way to do it, and why we must be wild to suggest doing something out of the norm.

Honestly, I didn't even know it would be strange to take a six-month-old camping for the first time. The weather was getting warmer, camping season was about to start, and my husband and I were excited to share our love of nature with our kiddo. So we told people our plan.

That was a mistake.

I was not ready for all of the fear and doubt coming my way. People told me their camping horror stories, *"This one time ... "* They asked questions that sounded a lot like accusations, *"Is it even healthy for a child to be outside all night like that?"* They questioned my sanity, *"Are you crazy? I would never take a baby that little camping."* There were more questions than I knew what to do with, *"What if he gets sick? What if he wakes up the whole campground? What if you forget something you need? What if there are bears?"*

Their words started to get to me.

- *Was I making a bad choice for my son?*

- *Would he be okay?*

- *Am I a bad mom for wanting to do this?*

I know parents struggle with these kinds of questions all the time. The weight of their judgment pressed down on me, making me feel small and uncertain. Their fear, projected onto my choices, felt like a judgment on my competence.

As a parent coach with a doctorate in child development, I knew what this really was. This was fear of the unknown, fear of things being out of your control, and fear of challenges.

It was time to apply my own critical thinking and problem-solving. Instead of accepting their fearful accusations, I decided to treat each one like a manageable roadblock. With all the noise about dirt, insects, and crying, my biggest questions became, *"How am I going to do this my way? How do I take control of the narrative?"*

I didn't need permission. I needed a plan.

I started to flip the scripts, challenging each fear with a rational response. This simple, grounding process is one you can use, too:

What will I do if he starts to cry at night? → I will try to soothe him. I can pack us up and we can go home if he is unhappy and uncomfortable. Going home is not failing; it is simply a choice I can make. I want joy, not stress.

What will I do about diapers? → Not a biggie. I will bring a garbage bag. Then toss them when we are done. Problem solved.

What if he eats dirt? → Yea, he does that already, even at home. Parenting is dirty. This is simply sleeping in a different, beautiful place.

How would I warm up his bottle? → We will use a portable bottle warmer. We will bring the solid foods he loves. He will have plenty of food.

As a parent coach, I spend my days helping others hear the quiet, knowledgeable voice beneath the noise. It was time to listen to my own. My child, my choice, my challenges. This was never about the perfect camping trip. This was a way to reclaim my right to decide what 'hard' meant for my family.

I drew a line in the sand. I stopped asking, *"Am I a bad mom?"* and started dreaming, *"How can this be a wonderful moment for my family?"*

It was decided. **Yes, I am going to do this joyfully!** Of course, parts might be hard, and that is how parenting *is!* Whether sleeping in a familiar crib or a tent, parts of parenting are messy, confusing, and require improvisation. I asked questions of the brave parents who had gone before me, instead of relying on those who were simply scared and wanted to keep us safe. I organized. I planned.

And it was spectacular. My kiddo bounced on my lap, was in awe of the campfire, tried his first marshmallow (loved it!), woke up to the songs of birds. Yes, he ate some dirt. We all survived. We all thrived.

As I write these words, he is older and on a camping trip right now. He loves being outside and those early experiences helped shape him.

To any parent who is being told, *"No, you can't possibly do that,"* I encourage you to:

1. Take a deep breath.
2. Ask yourself if it is totally true.
3. Then plan for how you possibly could.
4. Ask yourself, beyond surviving, how can I come out of this adventure happier, stronger, and more joyful?
5. Allow yourself permission to do it messy, to make mistakes, to have experiences, to enjoy your time as a parent. Even when it is hard. Especially when it is challenging.

Children become brave as they watch *you* be brave.

You can do hard things, parents. You can be the exception. **Now go do the thing they said you couldn't. You absolutely can!**

Dr. Erica Buchholz

Dr. Erica Buchholz is the expert who sees you, understands your journey, and brings the humor needed to make the mental load lighter. Leveraging her doctorate in Applied Developmental Psychology and over 20 years of intense work with families, she coaches parents directly on how to confidently step into a life free from the chaos of burnout.

This is powerful, compassionate support that empowers you to gain lasting energy, reignite your joy, and confidently claim your identity. Through her unique method of intentionally integrating laughter and play, Dr. Buchholz activates your creativity and equips you with practical emotional regulation tools that last. Ready to transform exhaustion into peace of mind and start fully enjoying your family? This is where your new beginning starts.

Connect with Dr. Erica at https://becomingplayful.com

CHAPTER 10

You Betcha I Can, and I Did!

Ewa Krempa

I dedicate this chapter to my daughter, Natalia. You are my greatest inspiration and reminder of why I dream big and live boldly. May you always know your worth, follow your heart with courage, and create a life filled with joy, freedom, and limitless possibility.

From the time I was young, I loved the idea of traveling. While other kids flipped through teen magazines, I found myself wandering into bookstores, losing hours in the travel section. I'd trace my fingers over the glossy covers of adventure guides, imagining myself in faraway places: hiking mountains, walking ancient streets, tasting exotic food. At first, it was just Europe, then Mexico, and soon my imagination had no limits.

But here's the thing: in my family, nobody had traveled the world extensively. No one had worked on a cruise ship or stepped outside the *expected path*. I was just a shy girl from a small village in Poland, later living in Edmonton, holding onto a secret dream.

Saying Yes to the First Big Leap

One day, I did something completely out of character. Against all odds, I applied for a job on a cruise ship. I knew nothing about that environment, the discipline, the demands, the lifestyle. To be honest, I didn't think I had much of a chance. But somehow, step by step, I passed through every requirement.

Before I knew it, I was stepping onto an Air Canada flight from Edmonton to the UK, leaving everything familiar behind. I was nervous, excited, and eager all at once. A friend of mine watched me walk away, whispering to herself, *She'll be back in no time.* But I wasn't. I was stepping into something that would change the way I saw life—and myself—forever.

Once I arrived in the UK, one final test awaited me. I'll never forget standing at the edge of a diving board high above the pool. I had to jump in and prove I could hold my own in the water. I wasn't a professional diver; in fact, I had never dived before. I only knew how to swim. But I hadn't come this far to give up. Deep down, I told myself: *YES, I CAN.* And I DID. I jumped before fear took over.

Working on a cruise ship opened a world I had only dreamed about in those bookstore aisles. Suddenly, I wasn't just reading about the world—I was living it. I circumnavigated the globe. I skydived, ziplined, dined in some of the most luxurious restaurants in Dubai, wandered through temples in Asia, walked along Caribbean beaches, and stood in awe before ancient cities. I explored corners of the world I never imagined I'd see.

The timid, shy girl from Poland became a woman with stories from over 50 countries. Travel reshaped me. It cracked open my shell and reminded me that courage isn't about not being afraid; it's about leaping anyway.

From Traveler to Storyteller

Years later, when my travels slowed, another dream started whispering to me: the dream of sharing my stories in writing. At first, it felt impossible. Who was I to write? English wasn't even my first language. But that same spark I had felt stepping onto that flight to the UK returned. *Why not me?*

So, I said YES again. I began writing in collaboration books, sharing my travel stories and the lessons I had learned along the way. The first time I held one of those books in my hands, I cried happy tears. Something that had once been just a shy dream had become reality.

And then came the bigger leap—the leap of building my own business. Once again, I had every reason to hesitate. I didn't know all the steps, I didn't have everything figured out, and the path ahead was uncertain. But I remembered the girl who had jumped off that diving board, the young woman who had stepped onto that flight to the UK, the traveler who had stood in awe on six continents. And I told myself once more: *YES, I CAN.*

That's how **Dynamic Mindset Solutions** was born. My business became not just a way to work for myself, but a way to help others rewire their thinking, reclaim their confidence, and create lives filled with purpose and freedom. I discovered that my calling wasn't just about my own adventures—it was about helping others find theirs.

Today, when I look back, I am proud of myself. From a little village in Poland to over 50 countries around the world. From shy and uncertain to **three-time international bestselling author.** From following other people's paths to carving out my own as a Transformational Mentor.

The Power of Decision, Clarity, and Gratitude

And here's the message I want you to take away: **your life changes the moment you DECIDE.** Every breakthrough I've experienced, from saying YES to the cruise ship, to jumping into that pool, to writing in a collaboration book, came from a single decision made with CLARITY. You don't need to see the entire staircase; you just need to take the first step with conviction. Decision-making is powerful because it closes the door on doubt. Once you decide, the path begins to reveal itself.

The second lesson is **CLARITY.** When you're clear on what you want, even if it starts as a quiet dream, you can move mountains. Clarity allows you to align your actions with your vision instead of scattering your energy in a hundred directions.

And third: **GRATITUDE.** Gratitude has carried me through every stage, gratitude for what I had, for what I was learning, and, even more importantly, for what was still to come. Gratitude shifts your focus from scarcity to possibility, from fear to trust. It opens your heart to receive more than you ever imagined.

So, whether you feel stuck, small, or unsure of yourself, know this: if a shy girl from a village could go on to explore the world, write books, and build a business she loves, so can you.

You don't have to know all the steps. You just need the courage to make the **decision**, find **clarity** in your vision, and stay rooted in **gratitude** along the way.

Because the truth is this: **Yes, you can. And when you do—you'll look back and say with pride, just like I do now: Yes, I can. And I did.**

Ewa Krempa

Ewa Krempa is a dynamic entrepreneur, mindset author, and transformational mentor based in Alberta, Canada. A passionate traveler, she has explored over 50 countries—experiences that expanded her perspective and shaped her mission to inspire others to live boldly and create the life they truly desire.

As the founder and CEO of Dynamic Mindset Solutions, Ewa helps individuals at midlife and beyond break through limitations, cultivate clarity, and design lives of freedom, fulfillment, and impact. Drawing on her own journey—from a shy girl in a European village to building a thriving business and traveling the world—she guides clients to step into courage, transform their mindset, and embrace new possibilities. Today, she blends timeless wisdom with practical tools to help her clients thrive mentally, emotionally, spiritually, and financially.

Ewa is a three-time international bestselling author, featured in the books *Midlife Awakening*; *Never Give Up*; and *Ripple Effect of Impact*. She also leads community-based programs that create spaces for growth, connection, and transformation.

Through her podcast, books, and signature transformational programs, Ewa equips people with the tools and strategies for lasting change. Whether in group programs, one-on-one coaching, or live events, her mission is clear: to empower people to believe in themselves, take courageous action, and build the life and business they dream of.

Connect with Ewa Krempa https://linktr.ee/EwaKrempa.

CHAPTER 11

Sometimes

J.A. Owens

First and foremost, to my wife, Shantelle, for the
million little things.
And to my mentor in grad school, Michelle
Hawes, for planting the seed.

Sometimes, it's the things others tell us. Sometimes, it's the things we tell ourselves. Oftentimes, what we tell ourselves is couched in what others have been telling us. So, what you say, and what you do, make a difference. Words hurt, and words heal.

For decades, I lived with the painful words of others.

YOU'RE LAZY!

YOU CAN'T DO IT!

YOU'RE A NOBODY!

YOU'LL NEVER AMOUNT TO ANYTHING!

Words from family, teachers, and church leaders. The most painful from the ones I truly looked up to. Regardless of their origin, words can lead to hopelessness, or they can lead to hope.

I am intimately familiar with the specter of hopelessness. I was born into abject poverty. I carry the emotional and physical scars that are a constant reminder of where I came from. I was born into it. I was raised with it.

My entire childhood, and well into adulthood, was spent hearing the reframe of why we couldn't, why we can't, and why things were never going to be. And, I've work with families wrestling with hopelessness on a daily basis. I know what hopeless is. I know what hopelessness feels like.

But, for reasons I am still trying to understand, whether it be fate, Divine intervention, or what have you, I was plucked out of that environment, and was surrounded by people in my life who taught me what could be, what can be, and what will be – if I will just believe. They taught me HOPE – that HOPE TURNS THE CANNOTs OF OUR LIVES INTO THE CAN-DOs.

My wife, Shantelle, has been instrumental in teaching me that. Forever the optimist, every time that I was bogged down by life, stuck in the mire, and weighed down by old ideas that I can't, she was there, and continues to be there, with a gentle and hopeful nudge, "Of course you can."

If there was one area of my life that hopelessness reared its ugly head, over and over again, it would be school. Academics were a struggle. From about 3rd grade on, I felt like the proverbial fish out of water. So, in hindsight, it was no surprise to me that I barely graduated from high school with no prospects, no idea of what I was doing or where I was going, and no hope. College was the furthest thing from my mind.

Comments from my teachers and leaders only reinforced that hopelessness. One referred to it as the Peter Pan Syndrome – you are never going to grow up!

When we were married, my wife was completing her MBA. When we met, she had already earned her degree in accounting. I was almost a high school dropout. I have no idea why she wanted to marry me, but she did, and I am eternally grateful. I ask her often why she took a chance on me, and she always replies, in one form or another, "I saw you for you and what you could be, and not what you think you were and couldn't be." Those words hit home. They gave me hope then, and give me hope now.

The beauty of hope is that it is contagious. Hope always breeds hope, and it spreads. From my wife's gentle encouragement, I hesitantly enrolled in school, filled with doubt and uncertainty. I leaned a lot on my wife's hope during those early years. It took time for my hope to grow, but it did, and it multiplied.

Despite years of hearing why we couldn't go to school, that a degree was out of our reach, my mom, my sister, and I each graduated from college within a semester or two of each other. I graduated from grad school. My mom and sister were shortly behind with their own master's degrees. A few years later, I graduated from law school.

Since then, two of our children graduated from college at the top of their classes. Another sister is working on her degree, as well as my nephew. My niece graduated from a top-tier law school and her sister is working on her PhD.

Thirty years ago, if anyone would have asked me where I was going, or what my plans were, college would have been the last thing on my mind because I did not think I could do it. I did not think it was even the remotest of possibilities. But, because my wife planted, and nurtured that seed of hope, and reminded me often, "Of course you can," I learned to ignore the "Cannots" and focus on the "Can-Dos."

Again, sometimes, it's the things others tell us. Sometimes, it's the things we tell ourselves. Oftentimes, what we tell ourselves is couched in what others have been telling us – for worse, or for better.

I wanted to help others avoid those same painful words I had heard, and lived with, for so long – leading to hopelessness. I wanted to honor those who taught me different, to be a messenger of hope. I wanted to yell,

YES, YOU CAN!

YOU CAN DO IT!

IF I CAN DO IT, SO CAN YOU!

I recently had the privilege of hearing a former student of mine speak at a function for prospective law students. Danielle was a single mom, working, and attending school full time. She had been accepted into law school, a longtime dream of hers.

She spoke of her journey to get there. The work and the sacrifices she had to make. And then she said the most beautiful, and unexpected, thing I had ever heard. She turned to me, in the audience, and said, "I gave him every reason why I couldn't, and he gave me every reason why I could. Thank you, Professor Owens. I am going to law school because you said I could."

You never know how much impact that hope, or giving hope, to others will have. But, sometimes, things have a way of circling back, just to let you know, that you made a difference.

Jeff Owens

Jeff Owens has been married to his best friend for almost 30 years. He and his wife have three kids, and a puggle named Jelly Bean. He is an attorney, and is a practicing mediator, mentor, and trainer. In the evenings, Jeff teaches conflict resolution at a local university. He loves to spend time with his family, traveling, the outdoors, and is a huge movie-buff!

Connect with Jeff at <u>owensjeffreya@gmail.com</u>.

CHAPTER 12

Life Can Change In a Split Second

Jacalyn Price

I dedicate this chapter to my DAD, Wilfred Price. My mentor, my best friend. He always has a smile on his face, loves life and is 94 years young. Nothing seems to worry him, and he is easy to please.

Accident Scene

On November 29, 2018, at the age of 65, I was hit by a taxi in Raymond Terrace, Newcastle, while walking on a pedestrian crossing. I remember seeing the taxi coming and I stopped in the crossing. When the female middle-aged driver slowed down, I continued.

Next thing I knew, she was right beside me and hit my left leg. I went airborne yelling in fear.

I recall hitting the road on my right side and watching the taxi wheels go past me very close. At that moment I thought about how lucky I was not to be run over as well.

I set up in shock, my heart was racing, and unable to move my right arm. I wondered what other damage could have happened to my body.

A crowd of people came running towards me. I had no idea what would happen from this. I was lucky enough to be pushed aside. My Aunt Eve was looking after me, my guardian Angel. My old judo days must have helped me as I did a break fall, which is when you land on a surface, use your arm outstretched to take the fall.

Hospital and Diagnosis

The ambulance was called, and I was taken to John Hunter Hospital in Newcastle.

The taxi driver was pulling into a taxi rank just past the pedestrian crossing, and she said, "I'm sorry. I didn't see you." The police were called as well, and they discovered there was a dash cam in the taxi, so they had a record of what happened.

X-rays on my right arm showed my arm was broken in six places—twice in the shoulder, twice in the elbow, and twice in the wrist.

Mum, Dad and the family came to visit me in hospital. I was scheduled for surgery the next day. Even with a high pain threshold, I was in a great deal of pain. They gave me morphine and the green whistle which helped a lot to relieve the pain.

It took six hours to put my arm back together; I was lucky to keep it. I was covered in bruises all down my right side and spent 4 1/2 months in hospital. The fall affected my balance as well and it took a while to get it back.

Operations and Therapy

My first operation involved getting pins and plates in my shoulder and wrist plus wires and screws in my elbow. In July 2019, I needed a complete elbow replacement. Initially, I couldn't lift or hold a table tennis ball or even hold my right arm up. I needed help at home seven days a week for 12 months.

This involved help with showering, preparing meals, cleaning, shopping. I slept partly upright with a pillow under my right arm. I had to do physiotherapy and hydrotherapy plus have a counsellor during his time.

At home, I would put my hand in a container of rice and try and hold and squeeze the rice. I had a dish of warm water, and I would squeeze a sponge to have movement in my hand. At rehab, they had a range of exercises for me to strengthen my right hand and arm. I went to the hydrotherapy pool daily.

I learned the power of chakra healing, breathing techniques, meditation, yoga, exercises, emotional freedom technique (EFT) and the power of the subconscious mind. Now I don't need any pain relief medication other than Panadol occasionally.

Regaining Strength and Adaptation

I have lost 25% use of my right arm but that doesn't stop me. Initially, I had a weight limit of 2-3 kilos with my right arm for lifting, but over time I have gained more strength and now can lift around 4 kilos. I still have to be careful what I do.

It was my right arm (my dominant arm) that was injured. I had to learn to use my left arm for basic things like brushing my teeth, going to the bathroom and even writing. I learned to be ambidextrous, which is also good for brain function.

I couldn't drive for 12 months. My brother, Graham, put a knob on my steering wheel so I could drive with my left arm, and some sponge on my driver's door so I wouldn't bump my elbow, which was a great help.

The reflex sympathetic dystrophy (RSD) came back in my left foot due to injury from being hit by the taxi. RSD is an older term used to describe one form of complex regional pain syndrome (CRPS). Both RSD and CRPS are chronic conditions characterised by severe burning pain, nerve pain. I was initially on strong pain medication.

The doctor said, "You know how to deal with this and control the pain." Sometimes you need a reminder. Within a short period of time, I had no more RSD.

Our challenges make us stronger and being able to share my story with others makes a difference. Some challenges are small, some are big. Sometimes the smallest challenge can be the breaking point. I learned ways to deal with the challenge, using the power of the subconscious mind.

Closing Inspiration

Your subconscious mind learns through repetition, not logic. Tell it who you are until it has no choice but to believe. Start and end your day with gratitude.

I am so happy and grateful that …

- I woke up this morning
- I have a roof over my head
- I have food on the table

You never know when things will change.

Always be ready to be flexible in what and how you do things every day. Never take things for granted.

Magic is in your thoughts. If I can do it, so can you. I'm doing more now than I was 20 years ago.

"Courage is not the absence of fear, but the triumph over it." ~Helen Keller

---

YOUR STRENGTH isn't measured by what you went through, but in how you went through it.

May you never crumble with life's challenges, but allow them to teach you and bring you to higher places of understanding. You can, and you will triumph.

Jacalyn Price

Jacalyn Price is an award-winning businesswoman, international best-selling author, and passionate wellness advocate known as The Wise Water Woman.

After personally healing herself from chronic bronchitis in 2023 using Kangen water, Jacalyn became a powerful voice for natural, water-based wellness—transforming lives through education, hydration, and empowerment.

Founder of a thriving Enagic-Kangen Water business, Jacalyn is a two-time winner of ACN's (All Communications Network) Business of the Year for Business Services (2020 & 2021) and a highly sought-after speaker, mentor, and networker.

Her work and story have been featured in Bx Xclusive Magazine, Newcastle Weekly, Newcastle Herald, Women of Worth Magazine.

She was a featured guest for International Women's Day.

Jacalyn is a dynamic presence in Australia's business networking community.

She is recognized as a finalist in numerous prestigious awards including the Hunter Region Business Excellence Awards, Australian Small Business Champion Awards, Women in Business Connect Awards, Australian Women's Small Business Champion Awards, Australian Ladies in Business Initiative Awards, Local Business Awards, and Bx xCellence Awards.

Jacalyn credits her success to consistent personal growth and learning from leaders like Bob Proctor, Mary Morrissey, Jim Rohn, Tony Robbins, and Zig Ziglar.

Driven by a deeper purpose, Jacalyn is on a mission to create a future foundation to support individuals and families navigating serious illness—an initiative inspired by her sister Jen's cancer journey.

Jacalyn lives to touch hearts and change lives, one conversation, one drop of water, and one act of kindness at a time. Connect with Jacalyn at https://jacalynp.mlcwater.com.

CHAPTER 13

Breaking Free From the Golden Cage: The Silver Lining in the Pandemic

Latara Dragoo

To my daughter: may you learn from where I stumbled, rise where I fell, and always follow the fire of your own dream, never another's.

When the Dream Job Became a Cage

I had the career life. The dream job. The dream house. The dream car. Ironically, I even worked for *Dream Homes Magazine*. For 18 years.

What began as a dream gradually unraveled into an unspoken nightmare.

It's hard to explain if you haven't lived it: The way complacency seeps in, the way subtle oppression can erode you without you noticing. The Machiavellian atmosphere quietly infiltrated my psyche. The criticism, the office politics, the power plays, the silent disapproval that hums beneath the surface. They didn't break me all at once; they wore me down like waves on stone, eroding the edges of who I was. Somewhere along the way, my spirit began to dim.

My partner tells me I came home crying nearly every day, though at the time I didn't realize it. I only knew I wasn't happy. I felt hollow.

I spent more time with my coworkers than my own family. And when my daughter was born, that ache intensified. Every morning, I'd walk out the door to her sobs, feeling like I was tearing my heart from my own chest.

Then came a breaking point.

I was already drowning. My mother had passed, and I carried a guilt I couldn't shake. One day, I was verbally torn apart, not just by my boss, but by a coworker as well.

I felt myself folding in, retreating inside my own skin. The air felt heavy. My body moved on autopilot, grabbing my keys, sliding behind the wheel. My mind wasn't on the road; it was on the chaos inside my head. The bollard came out of nowhere, but the truth is, it didn't.

It was as if my internal chaos had manifested itself in the form of steel and concrete. The accident added more fuel to my resolve.

Over the years, I tried to build an escape plan. I launched a mom blog. I opened an online baby store. I tried side hustles that promised freedom but delivered only exhaustion. I even hired a website manager to help build my exit strategy. But nothing brought in enough to replace my paycheck, and walking away without a plan felt irresponsible. So I stayed. Year after year.

Losing Everything—And Finding Freedom

And then, everything changed. A global event that shook the entire world. For many, the Pandemic was a season of fear, loss, and uncertainty. For me, quietly and unexpectedly, it was my release.

I lost the dream job. Then the dream house. But in that loss, I found freedom.

I wasn't just a hobbyist entrepreneur anymore. I was the CEO of my own business. I set my own hours. I worked from home. I no longer had to leave my daughter crying at the door.

Five years later, I'm still figuring it out. Some months are lean. Some are abundant. But every single day, I know I'm building something for myself, on my terms.

What I Learned—and What It Might Mean for You

Looking back, I see that the crash (the literal one and the metaphorical one) wasn't just the end of a chapter. It was a reckoning.

We're taught to believe that security is worth the sacrifice, that staying in a job that drains us is a sign of responsibility. But here's the truth: there's a cost to that kind of safety, and it's often your soul.

I spent years telling myself I was being practical. That one day, when the timing was right, I'd leave. But life rarely hands us a perfect exit plan. Sometimes, the leap comes disguised as a loss or failure.

And here's the thing: Your freedom may not come in the same package mine did. It might not be a pandemic. It might not be a crash.

But it could be the slow realization that your life is not your own anymore.

If while reading this you're feeling that familiar ache, that knot in your stomach when you walk into work, that sense of being a stranger in your own life, then maybe this is your invitation.

You don't have to burn it all down tomorrow. In fact, I would even suggest NOT burning the boats and bridges providing your current stability. But you can start building something now, even in small ways, using your "why" to motivate you.

One brick. One step. One choice toward the life you actually want.

I used to think the dream was the job, the house, the car. Now I know the dream is waking up with a sense of peace and of having ownership over your days.

For me, it took losing everything I thought I wanted to find what I truly needed.

For you, maybe it's simply the courage to start.

Because one day, you'll look back, whether it's five years or twenty, and the question won't be, *"Did I have the dream job?"*

It will be: "Did I live my dream?"

And I hope your answer is yes.

Latara Dragoo

Helping thought leaders build legacy brands, Latara Dragoo is a seasoned Branding and Digital Marketing Strategist with more than 25 years of experience in marketing, graphic design, sales funnel creation, and online business growth. Having spent nearly two decades in luxury brand publishing, she brings a rare combination of creative vision and strategic expertise to every project.

As the founder of a successful marketing agency, Latara partners with heart-centered speakers, coaches, authors, and impact-driven entrepreneurs to build magnetic brands that resonate deeply with their audiences. Her mission is simple yet powerful: to help thought leaders bridge the gap between their big ideas and the people they're meant to serve—transforming visionary concepts into tangible, profitable realities.

Latara's approach blends creativity with proven strategy, empowering clients to cut through digital noise, stand out with confidence, and grow their businesses with clarity and ease. She specializes in creating powerful online presences that not only elevate visibility but also generate consistent leads and long-term impact.

Her clients often describe working with her as liberating because she removes the stress of technology while helping them establish brands as professional and polished as billion-dollar companies.

If you're ready to elevate your presence, create meaningful connections, and grow a brand that becomes your legacy, Latara Dragoo is the trusted guide to help you every step of the way.

Connect with Latara at https://idealmarketing-solutions.com.

CHAPTER 14

Rewriting 55 Years: The Journey Back to Me

Laura Richards

I dedicate this chapter to every woman who has ever felt invisible, silenced, or small. This is for you as you rise, reclaim your story, and return to yourself.

Living in the Shadows

I spent 32 years married to someone who was hard to figure out. He was the "nice" guy. He was well-liked in our community, even serving the homeless with his church on the weekends!

But at home, I walked on eggshells and never felt like I did anything that was good enough for him. He wasn't a "nice" guy to me.

He lacked empathy, he had a sense of entitlement, he had a constant need for admiration from me and everyone around him, and he had a need to control it all!

This is the classic definition of a covert narcissist. These characteristics cause untold suffering to partners that don't even realize what is happening to them. This was me for three decades. But now, I'm free!

Getting to this point in my story has not been easy, but it has been amazingly rewarding!

The Turning Point

In 2020, my mother passed away after a long illness, we had her funeral, and then, soon after, we went into lockdown. During that time, I also decided to leave my career as a speech therapist. In 2021, we had another tragedy happen when our sister-in-law passed away from the worldwide virus. The shock of it was too much for our family to bear. Months later, I was still understandably sad. I had never grieved like this before. My then-husband would come home from work, and ask me why I was *still* depressed and crying. I agreed with him, and decided that going to therapy would be the best thing for me to do, so that I could "get over" my grief. I had never experienced a loss this great, so I truly thought I should be "over it" by now.

In therapy I started to talk about not only my grief, but why my husband was so difficult. The deaths of my mother and sister-in-law were starting to show me what a truly apathetic person my husband was. For years I had felt like he was difficult, and that everything I did was wrong. I would talk to friends and go to counseling, but nothing ever seemed to help. Going to individual therapy truly helped me wrap my head around my circumstances, my overall unhappiness, and what I wanted from my life. It was there that I decided that I had had enough of his indifference towards me. 33 years together was more than I could handle. Therapy not only gave me the strength to leave my marriage, but it gave me the courage to look at myself and what I wanted out of life.

I started my healing journey with one focus in mind—who am I as a divorced woman? I needed to heal my broken heart. I needed to know who I was. I needed to learn healthy boundaries. I needed to rewrite the last 33 years.

Laura had no idea who she was. The choices I had made throughout my life were driven by the experiences of my past, including my childhood. As I started to heal, I learned that I really needed to rewrite and heal the last 55 years of my life. The journey was just beginning!

Thinking back to the time right after my divorce, I can say I was sad but I was proud of the tools I had for my healing. I was doing really well for about three months, and then a bombshell hit. It was then that I learned that he had been dating a former coworker. When I found out about her, my entire life flashed before my eyes, and I felt like the blindfold had been ripped off. I suddenly started seeing everything I needed to see about narcissistic abuse! When I heard that term, all of a sudden my entire marriage made sense. Every lie, every betrayal, every manipulation tactic, every single thing he had said about me, or how he had treated me suddenly became crystal clear.

I call this my second Day One! I dove even deeper into my healing. I learned all the terms. While they were painful to hear, learning them helped me to wrap my brain around what had happened to me. This helped me to feel understood, seen, and heard! The real healing could now begin!

I began looking for support in the community in the form of support groups and talking with friends, but was met with opposition. People I knew talked to me and told me I shouldn't talk about my ex or call what had happened to me abuse. This was confusing and made me feel very alone. I felt ashamed for speaking out about what had happened to me.

Even though many people told me not to talk about my abuse, I decided that I just couldn't do that. It didn't make sense to me. If I felt this alone, maybe there were others who felt this way as well. I wanted to share what I went through with others, so that they could see healing is possible!

Reclaiming My Voice

I had always loved helping women, and that dream never went away. Soon after my divorce, I employed a friend of mine who is a wellness coach to help me dream again. As I worked with my coach to help me dream again, I had a newfound freedom to dream as big as I wanted to.

I felt the need to create a community for women who were like me who felt alone in their journey after divorce. I dreamed of a podcast, and started talking to women all over the world about how they have healed. No more would we be quiet about the abuse that had happened to us!

My podcast is a hit, but my mission is where I keep my focus: to shine a light on narcissistic abuse and let women know they are never alone and that healing is always possible.

I now live my life by the motto of, "Yes, I can and I did!"

Laura Richards

Laura Richards is an international podcaster, #1 bestselling author, and speaker dedicated to empowering women. Through her global podcast, "That's Where I'm At," and her bestselling book *"Married To A "Nice" Guy: Getting Over Narcissistic Abuse*," Laura shares her personal journey of recovery from a 32-year marriage to a narcissist.

Drawing from her own experiences, Laura's mission is simple: to shine a light on narcissistic abuse and let women know they are never alone and that healing is always possible. With an unwavering commitment to truth, Laura helps women rebuild their self-worth, reclaim their voices, and step into a future filled with confidence and strength.

She is the mom of three grown children, a mother-in-law, and a grandmother who lives happily with her cat in her hometown of Las Vegas.

Connect with Laura at https://www.thatswhereimatpodcast.com

CHAPTER 15
Limitless Aletheia

Mary Gould

For every parent, child, and learner who seeks a voice:
this is for you. My daughter's Morse code journey
revealed that communication is limitless when fueled by
love and determination. May you find courage to create
pathways of understanding where words alone
seem impossible.

The room I woke up in was dark, but the hallway beyond the door was a glaring white. Busy figures in lab coats hurried by. No one paid any attention to me.

Where was I?

Eventually, someone stepped into the shadows of my room. "Good. You're awake," he said in a low voice. "What's your name?"

"Mary."

"How old are you?"

"32."

The rest of his questions were so obvious, they left me wondering if I was on an alien spaceship being pumped for information they'd use to take over the world. Why else would he want to know what year it was, who the president was, etc.?

But no, I was actually at Akron City Hospital after a stroke he said I'd had during my 30th week of pregnancy. I didn't remember any of it, but he said I'd had HELLP Syndrome and they'd had to do an emergency C-section.

I was released, more or less back to normal, after three weeks, but my precious 2-pound, 11-ounce daughter hadn't fared so well. The doctor said she'd had a grade IV intraventricular hemorrhage (a brain bleed that would probably keep her from walking).

But it did more than that. It kept her from talking, from moving her arms and hands intentionally, and from doing most anything one would expect from a child.

Our beautiful Aletheia Joy had cerebral palsy.

She lived up to her name, though, and brought everyone around her joy! Her smile was contagious, and I decided to be thankful for the blessings in our life, despite her many limitations, all the extra care she required, the many specialists we regularly saw, etc.

When her neurologist heard me speaking French to her, he discouraged exposure to more than one language.

"We don't even know if she'll master English," he said.

That was disappointing for me, having grown up in Europe and speaking multiple languages, but as in the face of all the other disappointments, I just hugged her, communicating unspeakably great love, and was thankful she understood that.

Aletheia couldn't crawl around—touching, examining, and exploring her world like other kids—so language acquisition didn't come easy for her as it did for most children. But the blessing of a mother's love would still birth more understanding than either of us could comprehend! Through untold hours of mommy-daughter time, we began breaking through the barriers to her understanding without even realizing it.

She loved songs, so I sang… a lot!

"Head and shoulders, knees and toes, knees and toes…" And to make her smile even more, I'd touch each body part as I sang. "Eyes and ears, and mouth and nose…"

Sometimes, feeling goofy, I'd say things like, "Is this your head?" tickling her knee.

"No, silly Mommy! That's not your head! That's your knee!" I'd answer for her.

And before I knew it, her little brain picked up on the difference between both questions and answers and things that are and are not.

However, no matter how hard I tried, "yes" and "no" remained a mystery to her Until, that is, her brain was ready for it.

One spring day just after her fourth birthday, she was sitting sideways across my lap, leaning back against my arm, which rested on the left arm of our cozy, brown couch. It was our favorite place to spend time together.

Looking out the window to my right, I couldn't help but be amazed at what I saw.

"Wow! Isn't this a beautiful day? The sun looks pretty shining through the trees, doesn't it? Don't you just love how green the leaves have gotten in the past couple weeks? The trees sure look a lot better now, huh?" I mused. "And isn't the sky such a gorgeous blue? Just look at those clouds. Don't they look just like feathers, floating up there? Looks like spring really is here now, huh?"

I wasn't expecting an answer; of course; I just happened to string together a bunch of questions. But as I was talking, I noticed she was tapping me with her nose after each question. And as I finished another question, again she pressed her nose to my left cheek.

"Are you doing that on purpose?"

"Yes," I felt her nose tell me on my cheek. I couldn't believe it!

"Aletheia, are these your toes?" I touched her ears, wondering if she had also figured out "no."

She touched me with her forehead.

She had just figured out an important part of communication, but I was left speechless!

And that was only the beginning:

After almost four weeks of "yes" and "no," I was blessed with a thought: adapting Morse code to her touches, so she could answer open-ended questions:

"What did you hear?" I might ask.

"C" for "car" or "B" for "bird," she could say.

I'd tried three times over the past year to teach her the alphabet, but she hadn't understood. But now she was more than ready.

I sang the Alphabet Song, which she knew, and flipped through big, red letters. Later, I showed them to her again, saying consonant and short and long vowel sounds. I looked up Morse code online and tapped out each letter on her nose and forehead.

She mastered the Morse code alphabet in three sittings.

"What's the first letter in 'cat'?" I then asked hopefully.

"C-A-T," came the response.

Um, oh. Uh, wow…!

"That's right! What about 'grape'?"

"G-R-A-P-E."

She even spelled "congregation" almost right: C-O-N-G-R-E-G-A-S-H-U-N—a mistake she only made once, before being told "-tion" is spelled strangely.

From words she progressed to sentences, and then to conversations.

Now Aletheia tells me whatever she wants. Her little brain broke through the communication barrier in its own way.

My Aletheia Joy is limitless.

Mary Gould

Mary Gould empowers foreign language learners to break through barriers and discover confidence in their new languages. Her own experiences adapting to life in three countries while developing competent communication skills have given her deep empathy for those navigating similar challenges.

As a teenager, Mary turned to languages to cope with culture shock and has since gone on to study 14 and explored several others, simply out of delight of discovery. Part of her studies involved earning a B.A. in English, a minor in Biblical Languages, and an M.A. in German Translation.

For over 20 years, Mary has been helping people from across the world strengthen their foreign language proficiency and broaden their cultural awareness. She poured herself into authoring several language-learning books and creating a variety of amusing language-focused products and has been rewarded with a sense of immense fulfilment.

However, she primarily serves the international community as a certified and accredited Neurolanguage Coach®. Her coaching practice, Language of Hope, is grounded in neuroscience, not only leveraging strategies that align with the brain's linguistic processing, retention, and development but also considering her coachees' emotional language barriers from past experience.

Mary specializes in equipping speakers of multiple languages to deepen understanding, express themselves more freely, and sustain their enthusiasm for continued growth. Through her coaching, books, and other creative resources, Mary's mission is to inspire others to experience the freedom and hope that come from communicating effectively across cultures.

Connect with Mary at https://LanguageOfHope.Life.

CHAPTER 16

You Are the Architect of Your Becoming

Nasirra R Ahamed

To those who whispered "no," to those who dared to say "yes," and to my son, Roshan, who lights my world: may this story be a spark, a mirror, and a bridge—awakening your courage, illuminating your freedom, and revealing the infinite possibilities that always live within you. Mama loves you!

I was not born brave.

I was the quiet one in the corner, the one who watched more than she spoke. The one who had a thousand thoughts but never the courage to give them a voice. I was the girl who was told what she could and couldn't do, not because the world was cruel, but because it was conditioned.

As a little girl, I remember sitting beside my grandmother, Mummy Jan, listening to the rhythmic sound of her prayer beads. Between verses of faith, she told me stories of women who lived quiet lives of service and sacrifice. I loved her deeply, but even then, I knew my path would be different. I wanted to serve too, but in my own voice, my own way.

I grew up believing that success came only if you chose the right label, the right job, if you looked and spoke a certain way. Anything else was a detour. My story began with invisible lines drawn around what I could and couldn't be.

But light has a strange way of finding its way through cracks.

Somewhere deep inside, I always believed I was meant for more, though I didn't yet know what "more" meant. My mother, Rehana, was my quiet strength. My father, Shafiq, was the steady ground beneath my feet. My brother, Nizam, stood beside me, even when I hadn't yet found my voice. They didn't give me wings; they gave me roots. And from those roots, I learned how to grow my own wings.

When I married Captain Radhakrishna, I was told that crossing religious lines would make life harder. It didn't. It made life real. Together, we built a home filled with laughter, love, and our son, Roshan, a light that makes every "no" I ever heard worthwhile.

People have often asked me, "How did you do it?"

The truth is I didn't always know what I was doing. I just knew I couldn't keep living by someone else's script. Every "you can't" became the ignition for my "I will."

When someone once told me I couldn't start a podcast because my voice was too deep, I started *The Energy Architect Podcast*™ the very next day. That same voice now reaches ears across continents. It wasn't about proving anyone wrong; it was about proving myself right.

Over the years, I've been humbled by global recognitions—being named among the Top 50 Under 50 and Top 10 Successful Indian Personalities by *India Today* and more than 117 others. But what means the most to me isn't the applause; it's the quiet peace that comes from knowing I chose myself... again and again.

The truth is, most of the battles we fight aren't outside. They're inside... in the invisible conversations between who we are and who we've been told to be. We inherit cultural and societal narratives without realizing how tightly they wrap around our thoughts.

When I began observing my own thoughts, not judging them, just watching, I started asking myself:

"Why am I thinking this?"

"Is this thought helping me or harming me?"

"Is it mine? Or something I was taught to believe?"

That's when everything shifted.

I began to see that most of our self-doubt doesn't belong to us. It's borrowed from culture, from family, from fear. The weight we carry isn't always ours to hold. Awareness is like turning on a light in a dark room. For years, I was stumbling over invisible furniture... guilt, fear, expectations. Once I switched on the light, I realized I could simply move around them.

We are not taught how much power we have over our own thoughts. We are taught to follow, to fit into patterns that someone else drew. But if you were born whole, complete, and perfect—and you are—then the only thing that makes you feel less than that is the story you keep repeating.

So, start by giving yourself grace. You are not incomplete. You're just carrying too many borrowed beliefs.

The next time you catch yourself thinking, "I'm not enough," pause and ask: "Who told me that?"

When you feel guilty for resting or ashamed for dreaming, pause again: "Whose voice is that?"

Maybe it's an old teacher who doubted you.

Maybe it's a relative's offhand comment.

Maybe it's society whispering rules that no longer serve you.

Once you see the source, you can unhook from it. Because awareness, my friend, is freedom.

If I could learn to see my own patterns, the ones that kept me small and lovingly rewrite them, so can you.

If I could walk from silence to self-expression, from fear to freedom, from being told I can't to standing here saying "I did," then you can, too.

Transformation doesn't happen overnight. It happens in quiet revolutions, in the moments you choose to notice, breathe, and respond differently. It's in catching yourself mid-thought and saying, "No, not this one. Not anymore." It's in forgiving the version of you who didn't know better and celebrating the one who's learning now.

Because life is not about what happens to you.

It's about what you choose to build from it.

And you—yes, you—are the architect of your destiny.

I often say that everything is energy. Our thoughts are frequencies. Our awareness is light. And destiny is not written in stone; it's sculpted through the energy we hold and the choices we make every single day.

When your awareness expands, your energy shifts.

When your energy shifts, your life begins to rearrange itself to match who you've become.

You don't need to fix yourself. You just need to wake up to yourself.

You don't need to chase power. You already are power—once you stop giving it away to the thoughts that limit you. And you don't need permission to begin again.

If I could speak to that quiet, underconfident girl I once was, I'd tell her this:

- You are allowed to dream outside the lines.
- You are allowed to be both soft and strong.
- You are allowed to build a life that once felt impossible.

And so are you.

Because when you finally turn inward and meet your own light, the world outside rearranges itself to match that glow.

Awareness is energy.

Your Energy shapes your Destiny.

And destiny when built with courage, consciousness, and grace always whispers back,

"Yes, you can. And yes, you did."

Nasirra R Ahamed

Nasirra R Ahamed is a two-time #1 International Best-Selling Author, ICF Certified PCC Life & Leadership Coach, Speaker, Mentor, and the Founder & Chief Coach of The Energy Architect™.

With over 26 years of corporate and global leadership experience, Nasirra blends spirituality, neuroscience insights, and psychology—anchored in both heart and strategy—to help leaders and individuals re-design their inner architecture. Her work focuses on clearing deep-seated emotional patterns, expanding awareness, and guiding people to rise into conscious, authentic versions of themselves.

Before founding The Energy Architect™, Nasirra held senior leadership positions across leading media and corporate organizations, building high-performing teams, shaping inclusive cultures, and driving transformative business growth. Her coaching practice today spans Asia, Australia, the US, the UK, and the Middle East—bringing a global yet deeply human approach to leadership, mindset, and transformation.

As a mentor to students at some of India's top B-Schools, Nasirra is passionate about shaping the next generation of emotionally intelligent and purpose-centered leaders through reflective and experiential learning.

Recognized among India's Top 10 Successful Personalities and Top 50 Under 50, Nasirra's insights have been featured in over 117 publications, including *Business Standard*, *The Print*, and *ANI N*ews. Through The Energy Architect™, she continues to bridge energy, neuroscience, and leadership—creating spaces where awareness becomes action and growth becomes lasting transformation.

Connect with Nasirra at https://www.nasirra.com

CHAPTER 17

My Story of Breaking Free from Scarcity

Niki Hall

From Hustle to Exhaustion

There was a time in my life when the end of every month felt like a relentless race. I would push hard, running to meet one deadline after the next, trying to squeeze every last bit of work in so I could deliver on time and meet all my financial obligations.

And you know what? Life never really let me down. Ever! The money always showed up somehow. The bills got paid. But deep inside, there was always this gnawing anxiety, a constant whisper saying, *"You're going to make it. Just like you have every other month."*

At first, that whisper felt encouraging, almost comforting, proving to myself that I was resilient, that I could figure things out. But over time, it became exhausting. It was as though my nervous system was living on high alert, month after month, year after year. There was no peace, no sense of breathing room.

Deep down, I knew this wasn't "how life was meant to be for me." This way of living; pushing hard, surviving, barely catching my breath before doing it all over again was unsustainable. Something had to change.

A Weekend That Changed Everything

Then came a weekend that changed everything. I attended a workshop that felt as though it had been written just for me. Every word landed. Every story felt like my story. Every teaching struck me like a bell ringing inside my heart. By the end of the weekend, I was no longer the same person who had walked into that seminar on Friday night.

That weekend gave me a clarity I had never experienced before. It was as though someone had turned on the lights in a room I had been stumbling through in the dark for years. I finally saw what I had been doing to myself; the fear-driven decisions, the limiting beliefs, the way I kept recreating the same month-to-month pattern without even realizing it.

And that weekend, I made a powerful decision:

I will never again live by default. I will create the life I want, and I will learn how to think, act, and believe like the person I see I am capable of being.

From that moment forward, I became the guardian of my thoughts.

Whenever I heard the old story creep back in, "I can't afford it," "This is just how life is," "I'll never get ahead," I stopped myself in my tracks and asked better questions:

- *"What if I could afford it?"*

- *"What would I choose if I knew I was supported?"*

- *"What would the next-level version of me do right now?"*

Those questions became my power tools. They helped me disrupt the old patterns and replace them with thoughts that opened doors instead of closing them. I didn't just think differently, I felt differently. I stood taller. I breathed deeper. And slowly, but surely, life began to respond in a new way.

Stepping Into Abundance

As my thinking shifted, I couldn't keep it to myself. I started sharing. First with close friends over coffee, then on social media, then in small groups. Everything I was learning about mindset, possibility, and personal power.

I spoke with passion, because I had lived the pain and lifestyle of scarcity. I wanted others to know there was a way out for them as well. Those first conversations lit a spark that would eventually become the foundation of my work today. The more I shared, the more I realized this wasn't just my journey, it was a calling. It was my calling.

Soon, my little side business began to grow into something more. I made the decision to stop treating it like a hobby and start running it like a real business. I invested in business courses. I hired coaches and mentors. I learned about marketing, branding, and building a client experience that truly delivered value.

The result of all of this is that I became the CEO of my own life, not just in business, but in how I made decisions, handled money, and saw myself.

With the guidance of a financial advisor, I started putting my money to work instead of just working for money. I began seeing money as energy, something that flows when you are aligned, something that grows when you treat it with respect.

Along the way, I discovered something beautiful: the first step to receiving is giving. When I began to create from a place of service, to truly pour into others, to give value, to share my heart, my entire life shifted.

I created programs that were not just about information, but transformation. I even created opportunities for those who couldn't afford to work with me right away, because I knew if I could help them break through, they would go on to change their world too. It was then that I realized: abundance is not just about having more. It's about being more. It's about being a source of good, a channel through which others can grow.

The more I lived this way, the more the flow opened up. Clients started coming to me with ease. Not because I was hustling harder, but because I was living in alignment with the life I desired. I was no longer living to meet these crazy, intense month-end goals. I was living in harmony with them, embodying the vibration of the wish fulfilled and becoming the person I already knew I could be.

This is what Bob Proctor and Mary Morrissey, two of my many mentors, taught me: you must live *from* the dream, not *toward* it. You must work from within, not from the outside in.

I made that dynamic shift. I began to see that the Universe responds to how we feel, not just what we do. When I showed up each day with faith, gratitude, and purpose, the right people, opportunities, and resources flowed into my life.

I wasn't chasing anymore. I am now attracting. And that feels incredible.

Today, I look back and see how every step, every decision, every mindset shift built the bridge from where I was to where I am now. Shifting your money mindset isn't just about money. It's about freedom. It's about health. It's about happiness.

It's about saying with confidence:

And if I can do it, so can you!

Niki Hall

Niki Hall is a passionate Mindset and Success Coach who helps people break through limitations and step boldly into their potential.

From a young age, Niki discovered her ability to inspire and empower others, even launching a self-help school early in life. Later, she became the author of *Building Up – Thoughts Expressed During the Readjustment of Self*, a powerful book on change and self-actualization that sold out its first printing within days. The book's success propelled her into public speaking and leading transformational workshops.

In 2021, Niki expanded her work by coaching entrepreneurs and professionals to take inspired action, elevate their lifestyles, and achieve their full potential. Her mission is simple yet powerful: to help individuals create more health, wealth, and fulfillment by mastering their mindset and applying it to everyday life.

Since 2023, Niki has participated in five compilation books where all five books have reached the #1 International Bestselling status. Her stories speak of empowerment as she shares practical insights on growth, mindset, and creating a life of purpose and prosperity.

If you're ready to take the next step toward your goals, Niki invites you to connect for a free 30-minute strategy call.

Book your session with Niki today at calendly.com/nikihallthrive.

CHAPTER 18

Say YES

Pearl Chiarenza

---

*Hey beautiful, this is for you — the woman who's always
shown up for everyone else but forgot herself along the
way. I see your strength, your heart, your exhaustion.
Remember, saying no isn't selfish — it's self-love.
Here's to you finding peace, joy, and the courage to say,
"Yes, I can."*

For most of my life, I was the dependable "yes" girl, the mom, wife, volunteer, and friend who made sure everyone else was happy. Saying no felt selfish. I thought that being helpful meant being worthy. The more I gave, the more I lost myself. I didn't realize how deeply I had buried my own dreams beneath everyone else's expectations.

A few years ago, I enrolled in a class called *Identity and Destiny*. I thought it would be a fun self-development course, but it turned out to be a mirror. Week after week, I was invited to look beyond my titles of mother, wife, daughter, friend and answer one question that shook me to my core: **Who am I without my roles?**

When I couldn't find an answer, I realized how much of my life had been lived for others. My worth had been wrapped up in being needed. One of my classmates said to me, "Pearl, I still hear all your titles and wonder who you really are?" That single sentence planted a seed of change inside me.

The very next morning, on my way to a networking meeting, I noticed a small rock on the ground. I don't know why I picked it up, but when I did, I felt grounded, like something solid reminded me that I could stand firm. That rock became my personal anchor, a daily reminder to stay rooted in who I was becoming.

That day, I made a promise to myself: I would say **"no"** at least three times a day. If I didn't find someone or something to say no to, I had to call, text, or email someone and practice it anyway. It might sound silly, but for a lifelong people-pleaser, it was revolutionary. I needed to retrain my brain and my heart, to believe that my voice mattered too.

The first few times were uncomfortable. I'd hang up the phone and feel guilty. My mind raced with thoughts like, *What if they're upset? What if they think I'm selfish?* But the more I practiced, the more empowered I felt. Every "no" built a new kind of strength, the kind that comes from alignment, not approval.

I noticed something beautiful: each time I said no to something that drained me, I made space for something that fueled me. It wasn't rejection; it was redirection.

Then came the moment that forever sealed this truth in my heart.

Two days before my son Matt's car accident, he was in the garage working with his dad on their family business. I walked out to check on them, and he called over, "Hey Mom, throw me a bottle of water!"

Now, I have never been much of a thrower. I couldn't throw a football to save my life, and we used to laugh about it when he was younger. But this time, I grabbed the bottle, took a breath, and tossed it right to him. It landed perfectly in his hands. He laughed and said, "Man, Mom, not only have you figured out your stuff, but you can finally throw something!"

We all laughed, not realizing the weight those words would carry.

When Matt passed away two days later, his words echoed in my heart. "You've figured out your stuff." In the middle of unbearable loss, those words became a lifeline. They reminded me that before tragedy struck, I had already begun the work of reclaiming myself. I had started saying no. I had started healing. I had started living.

As I navigated my grief, I kept returning to the lessons I'd learned, the power of the rock, the boundaries, the rediscovery of self. Those lessons became the foundation for what I now call the **SHERO Method**, a pathway to becoming **Stronger, Happier, Empowered, Radiant, and Original**.

Stronger, because strength isn't about holding everything together; it's about knowing when to let go.

Happier, because joy isn't found in perfection; it's found in authenticity.

Empowered, because true power begins when we realize our "no" is just as sacred as our "yes."

Radiant, because when we stop dimming our light for others, we shine from the inside out.

And Original, because we were never meant to be carbon copies of everyone else's expectations.

Through the **SHERO Method**, I learned that self-care isn't selfish, it's necessary. I began leading retreats where women show up without makeup, without masks, and rediscover the parts of themselves they'd silenced for years. We talk, laugh, cry, and write our own permission slips to say yes to the lives we truly want. Watching women reclaim their power reminds me daily why I said yes to my own transformation.

That little rock still sits on my desk today. Every time I look at it, I remember the woman who was afraid to say no and the woman who finally did. I remember that I can be both kind and firm, loving and strong, giving, and grounded. Saying no didn't make me less caring; it made me more authentic.

If you're reading this and feeling torn between who you are and who everyone expects you to be, know this: you're not alone. Start small. Pick up your own "rock," something that symbolizes your commitment to yourself. Every time you're tempted to say yes out of guilt or fear, hold that rock and ask, *Does this honor me?*

If the answer is no, give yourself permission to choose peace instead of pressure.

Because here's the truth: when you stop saying yes to everything that drains you, you finally have the energy to say yes to everything that fulfills you.

So, say it with me: **Yes, I can. And I did.** And so can you.

If these words speak to your heart, I'd love to help you begin your own journey of becoming Stronger, Happier, Empowered, Radiant, and Original.

Join me for a cup of tea by downloading the QR Code in my bio on the next page.

Pearl Chiarenza

Pearl Chiarenza is a Say YES to Your Life™ Coach, speaker, and founder of Women's Successful Living, where she helps women stop people-pleasing and start living with purpose, joy, and confidence. Through her signature SHERO Method—which empowers women to become Stronger, Happier, Empowered, Radiant, and Original—Pearl guides clients to set guilt-free boundaries, rediscover their true selves, and say "no" as proudly as they say "yes." She is also the creator of the Soulful Self-Care PJ Retreats, where women unplug, release expectations, and reconnect to who they are beyond their titles.

Connect with Pearl:

🌐 www.WSLiving.com

✉ coachpearl@WSLiving.com

📱 Instagram & Facebook: @Pearl Chiarenza

Scan me

CHAPTER 19

Lessons Without Classroom

Salman Sarwar

I was born into poverty—a fact that may not sound extraordinary in itself, but in a country like Pakistan, being poor often feels like carrying a burden heavier than sin. From the very beginning, curiosity burned within me. I wanted to know how the world worked, what lay beyond the walls of our small home, and how people made something of themselves. But I had no idea where to begin. My father passed away when I was young, and in our society, child labor was hardly considered a problem. School became a distant dream. That's why I call this chapter *"Lessons Without Classrooms."*

The British Raj had left behind more than just architecture and systems—it had left behind two distinct classes. One belonged to those with money, who could afford good education, speak fluent English, and secure top positions in government or private offices. The other class was for people like me, who didn't even know how to compete with them. When you have no money, education seems like a luxury. I spent my teenage years wondering if I'd ever find a way out. But somewhere deep inside, the fire to change my circumstances refused to die.

In Pakistan, learning English is not just about learning a language—it's like deciding to teach yourself Spanish or Portuguese without a teacher, simply because your future depends on it. It's the only way to be taken seriously, to get a good job, to support your family. I didn't have a school or a tutor, but I had determination.

It started with second-hand books. I bought old English learning guides that had Urdu translations printed alongside. I studied at night under dim lights, fighting sleep and self-doubt. My relatives and friends laughed at me. They said no one had ever done it on their own—that it was impossible. But every time someone told me "you can't," it fueled me even more.

Around that time, I discovered English movies, and one of them changed my life forever—*The Shawshank Redemption*. I couldn't understand the dialogues at first, but a friend helped me translate bits and pieces. When I finally grasped the ending—when Andy crawled through despair and came out free on the other side—it struck me like lightning. If he could do that, then so could I. That movie didn't just entertain me; it redefined my belief in hope.

By the mid-1990s, computers began to enter Pakistan, and I set my sights on learning them. But again, there was the same wall—money. I couldn't afford school, classes, or even a computer. That's when my late mother, my angel on earth, gave me some of her savings so I could buy one. It had no internet, but to me, it was a window to a whole new world.

One day, while browsing through old bookstores again, I found a book on *Adobe Photoshop*. That moment changed my destiny. The book was full of pictures and examples, which helped me understand even with my weak English. I stayed up nights again, experimenting, practicing, failing, and trying again. My relatives mocked me, saying I was wasting my time. But two women stood by me unwaveringly— my mother, who never questioned what I was doing but believed in me, and my childhood friend Jasmine, who later became my wife.

Both of them shared the same name, and both were blessings from God. My mother passed away ten years ago, but her faith in me lives on through every success I achieve.

After marrying Jasmine, I faced another challenge—finding a job. I had no degree, no formal qualification, but I had skills and hunger. I finally got a job at a printing press—but as a tea boy. It was humiliating at first, but I needed the income. Then one day, fate knocked again. The company's designer was absent, and a project deadline was approaching. I stepped forward and said, "I can do it."

Everyone laughed, thinking it was a joke. But the owner, perhaps out of desperation, let me try. I sat at the computer and did the work. When he saw the final result, he was stunned. That single moment changed everything. My employer began to notice my dedication— my habit of staying up late, my eagerness to learn. He didn't know that every night, I was secretly teaching myself the craft I loved.

Soon after, I was offered a position at an advertising agency based purely on my work, not my degrees. I spent the next 18 years there, pouring my heart and creativity into everything I did. My boss even bought me an Apple Mac computer and asked, "Can you handle it?" I smiled and said, "Why not? I've handled tougher things." Within a month, I had mastered it.

Then came 2020. The COVID-19 pandemic hit the world like a storm, shutting down businesses and taking away livelihoods. I lost my job, too. But life had trained me never to sit idle. I turned to online freelancing—a completely new world, but one that offered limitless opportunity. It wasn't easy, and it still isn't, but my persistence paid off. I began getting work, slowly at first, then steadily.

Eventually, I had the honor of working with well-known clients like Lynda Sunshine West and Sally Larkin Green, two incredible women who noticed my dedication and gave me a platform to grow internationally. Each project reminded me of that poor boy who once couldn't afford schoolbooks. Each success whispered the same truth: *You can, and you did.*

When I look back now, I don't see a life of hardship—I see a life of lessons. Every failure taught me something that no classroom could have. Every "no" from others pushed me closer to a "yes" within myself. I never had teachers, but I had passion. I never had mentors, but I had examples of perseverance. And I never had comfort, but I had conviction.

My story isn't about overnight success or luck. It's about faith, resilience, and the quiet power of believing in yourself when no one else does. I hope that anyone reading this—especially those who think they're too poor, too uneducated, or too late—will understand one thing: *no effort ever goes to waste.* Every page you read, every hour you practice, every tear you shed builds the person you're meant to become.

I didn't just dream of change—I chased it, stumbled, and kept going until it became real. The boy who couldn't go to school now helps authors design their book covers across the world. The child who once watched *The Shawshank Redemption* without understanding a word now communicates with clients from America to Europe.

So, if life ever tells you that you can't, look in the mirror and say, "Yes, I can." Because if I did, so can you.

Salman Sarwar

Salman Sarwar, known professionally as Sam, is a freelance designer, art director, and book cover specialist whose journey from humble beginnings to international recognition is a story of resilience and creativity. Born and raised in Pakistan, Sam discovered his passion for learning and design without the benefit of formal education. Through sheer determination, he taught himself English, computer skills, and digital design—skills that would later define his career.

Over the years, Sam has collaborated with authors and publishers around the world, helping them transform their words into powerful visual stories. His work reflects not only technical mastery but also deep emotional understanding—an ability to connect art with meaning.

Behind every design, there is a personal story of persistence. Sam's path was shaped by challenges that once seemed insurmountable, yet each obstacle became a steppingstone toward his dreams. Today, he continues to push creative boundaries, believing that passion and perseverance can turn any limitation into opportunity.

Away from the screen, Sam is a proud father, a devoted husband to Jasmine, and a dog lover who believes life's greatest joys often come from its simplest moments. Though his world is small, his imagination remains boundless. He lives by a simple truth that defines his life and work: "Yes, I can—and I did."

Connect with Sam at

https://web.facebook.com/muhammad.salman.sarwar786

CHAPTER 20

MLMs Are a Scam—Nobody Makes Money

Sherri Renae Leopold

To every woman who has ever questioned her value: May you always remember you are an unrepeatable miracle exactly as you are—no qualifiers! Stand UP and stand OUT! Choose to be exceptional! I believe in YOU!

Saying Yes to a New Possibility

When I first stepped into the world of direct sales and network marketing in 1998, I wasn't chasing six figures, exotic vacations, or shiny car bonuses. My goal was much simpler: I wanted just a little extra money each month—money not already earmarked for bills, groceries, or the family budget. Just a few extra dollars—the kind that could pay for a family outing, a holiday, or a pair of shoes for the kids when they went on sale. That's all I wanted.

What I didn't know then was that my simple "yes" would change the trajectory of my entire life.

I had heard all the noise. "It's a scam." "It's a pyramid." "Nobody really makes money with those things." People around me didn't think it was a "real" job. Instead of letting their doubts define my path, I leaned in. I decided to see for myself what was possible. I chose to focus on what I could accomplish, not what others told me I couldn't.

Fast forward 27 years, and I can say with confidence: Yes, I can, and I did.

I have built teams of thousands. I've earned six figures and helped others create incomes that changed their families' lives. I've enjoyed company-paid trips to destinations I once only dreamed about. For more than 11 years, I've consistently earned an auto bonus every month, which means a car payment hasn't been my responsibility in over a decade. Most importantly, I've become my own boss. I design my days around what matters most to me.

That's not luck or hype. That's not "getting in early" or being the exception. It's the product of showing up, staying consistent, and building self-belief.

When I started, there was no vision board with cars and mansions. I wasn't trying to retire my husband or hit a million dollars in commissions. I was a mom looking to make life a little easier. One of the most important lessons I've learned: don't discount the power of small beginnings.

The extra $300-$500 a month that people laugh at as "not worth the time" is exactly what changes families. That money pays for sports fees, music lessons, groceries, or date nights. For some, it keeps the lights on. This still drives me today.

Not everyone was cheering me on. Some rolled their eyes. Others whispered that I was wasting my time. I heard the same tired comments: "Oh, one of those things." "That's just a pyramid scheme." It hurt. I quickly realized people react from their own experience. Their comments were simply a reflection of their own lack of expertise. What mattered was what I believed, and what I was willing to work for.

Travel incentives appealed to me. Since 1998, I've earned 31 trips. Each one proves that when you say yes and show up, doors open you never imagined walking through. It's proof to the naysayers: Yes, I can, and I did.

The first time I earned the company car bonus, I cried—not because of the car, but because it represented consistency, resilience, and recognition. It was my tenth company and took 15 years to figure out how to achieve it. Once I did, I never looked back. I've maintained that bonus for over 11 years. That's not a fluke—that's perseverance.

I didn't set out to earn six figures, but I did. I learned to lead, mentor, and duplicate success and build massive teams. Along the way, I became a stronger version of myself. I learned how to Stand UP and Stand OUT as the unrepeatable miracle I am.

To be clear, this isn't easy money. Success isn't quick. Many people quit before they ever see the fruit of their labor. Network marketing is simple, but it isn't effortless.

It requires consistency—showing up when it's inconvenient, following up when you don't feel like it, and doing the work daily. It requires **resilience**—being willing to face rejection, not take it personally, and keep going regardless. It requires **belief**—first in the product, and opportunity, but most importantly, in yourself. And it requires **community**—surrounding yourself with growth-minded people and lifting others as you climb.

These are the qualities that separate those who dabble from those who build legacies.

Lessons From Nearly Three Decades

Looking back on nearly three decades, here are the lessons that matter most. Start small, but start. Don't wait for the perfect moment. It doesn't exist. Celebrate the small wins. That first customer, that first rank advancement, even my first check—just $21—proved it worked. Detach from opinions. The loudest critics are those who never tried or lack commitment. Invest in yourself. The person you become on this journey is more valuable than the paycheck.

Never quit during a temporary defeat. Success comes from riding them out, not running from them.

Today, I wake up every morning knowing I am my own boss. I work for myself, not for someone else's dream. I don't ask permission to take a vacation, attend an event, or design my life. Did I believe this was possible when I started with that tiny dream of "just a little extra money"? No. But I kept saying yes, kept showing up, and kept proving to myself that I could.

I am proof that when someone says, "Nobody makes money in that," you can smile and know better.

This chapter isn't about me. It's about possibility. It's about what can happen when you choose to ignore the noise and pursue your own path.

I started with small hopes and built something extraordinary. I faced doubt and criticism, and I kept going anyway. I earned bonuses, trips, and income that changed my life.

The Power of Belief

Remember Roger Bannister, the man who broke the four-minute mile? Experts said it was impossible—until he proved it wasn't. He understood: IM possible. The moment he did, countless others followed, because the barrier was never the body, it was belief.

What do you believe is possible?

As for me, I told myself… Yes, I can, and I did!

Sherri Leopold

Sherri Leopold, CEO of Option Creators INC, is a Mentor, and Leader of the Stop Self-Bullying Movement. She is also the founder of the WOW WARRIOR Network, publisher of WOW WARRIOR Magazine, and host of the shows WOW WARRIOR and WOW—Look Who's Here!

Sherri is a 13-time International bestselling author. She is currently an Ambassador Mentor Candidate, a Regional Director Candidate and first ever National Trainer Candidate with Givers University. In addition, she has 27 years in Network Marketing/Direct Sales and experience in speaking, mentoring, and team building. She can help you transform your life mentally, physically, and financially through falling in love with yourself first.

Connect with Sherri at https://SherriLeopold.com.

CHAPTER 21

When It Rains, It Pours...Life's Steppingstones to Finding Your Greater Purpose

Tiffiny Jewel Roper

This book is dedicated to my girls, Avery and Sophia, and my late Dad, Ronnie. You girls inspire me to be the best mom I can be! I adore everything about the two of you and love you with all my heart! Dad, I am me because there was you.

When the Storm Hit

There are moments in life when the weight of the world seems to collapse on us all at once. For me, that season came like a storm I never saw coming. In the span of a little over a year, I endured losses and battles that would have brought anyone to their knees, and for a while, they brought me to mine.

I spent more than four years fighting to bring life into this world, a want I had felt at my core since I was a little girl—being a Mom. The fertility journey can be very lonely, going through treatments with a lot of hope and heartbreak, of longing and waiting, of prayers whispered late at night when no one else hears. When I finally became pregnant with twins, my heart swelled with joy, only to be shattered when they were born too early and died in my arms, as all I could do was watch helplessly. No amount of preparation could have prepared me for the pain of holding their tiny, fragile bodies, knowing that their lives had ended before they had truly begun.

As if that loss wasn't enough, life seemed determined to test me further. Less than two months before my twin daughters (my miracle rainbow babies) were born, my father passed away. He never had the chance to meet them, to hold them, to see the family I had fought so hard to build. I was soon celebrating new life while mourning the loss of the man who had given me mine while showing me what it was to be an amazing parent.

But the storm wasn't over yet. Only days after delivering my daughters, I received a diagnosis that would alter the course of my life again—postpartum cardiomyopathy, a heart condition that left doctors looking at me not with hope, but with statistics. "You won't live another five years without a transplant," they said. "And with one, you might have another five years." Their words echoed in my mind like a death sentence. According to them, I wouldn't live long enough to see my girls turn ten.

I remember sitting there, newborn twins depending on me, recovering from a C-section, and feeling like the walls were closing in. Not only was I facing grief and loss, but now I was staring down the reality of raising two babies while fighting for my own life. The medications I was prescribed meant I couldn't breastfeed or exercise, in fear of passing out. I felt robbed of the natural ways I had hoped to nurture my daughters and rebuild my strength. It was as though everything I had envisioned for this season of motherhood had been taken from me before it even began.

Choosing to Fight for My Life

But somewhere in that darkness, a small spark lit up inside me. A voice that whispered, *"This is not the end. You were made for more than just surviving. You will thrive."* Maybe it was the whispers of God, maybe the love from Dad.

That voice became my anchor. I realized that if I was going to defy the odds, it wouldn't be by focusing on the limitations placed on me by doctors or circumstances. It would be by choosing the right state of mind, every single day. And taking the necessary actions to get better while raising my beautiful girls.

I made a conscious decision: I would not let grief, fear, or medical predictions dictate the story of my life. I would raise my daughters not just to survive, but to thrive, and I would do it with my own heart beating strong inside me.

That didn't mean the journey was easy. Some days, the weight of exhaustion and fear threatened to crush me. There were nights when tears soaked my pillow as I grieved both the loss of my father and the twins I never got to watch grow up. But every time I looked at my daughters, I was reminded of why I had to keep going. They were my reason, my purpose, my proof that miracles happen even in the middle of the storm.

Slowly, I began to rebuild my strength, not just physically, but mentally and spiritually. I learned to master my internal state. To choose gratitude even when grief pulled at me. To choose joy even when fear whispered that my time was running out. To focus not on what I couldn't do, but on what I would do.

And over time, something extraordinary happened. My heart began to heal, not because of a transplant, but with my determination that I will listen to my own body, start exercising and slowly build my health back. I defied the prognosis, outliving every statistic the doctors gave me. I didn't just survive. I overcame.

Finding Purpose in the Pain

Today, I stand here raising beautiful, thriving twin daughters who fill my world with light and laughter. I've discovered a truth that changed everything for me: the storms in life aren't meant to destroy us. They are meant to refine us, to shape us into the people we were always meant to be. The struggles I went through, all within 13 months, could have broken me. But instead, it woke me up. It taught me resilience. It taught me compassion and grace—for myself and others. And, most importantly, it gave me a calling and purpose: helping others navigate their own storms. Because in life, we always have a choice in how we respond. We can let the storm drown us, or we can learn to dance in the rain.

I share my story now to empower you. So you know, no matter what, there is hope. And today, I choose to live with deep gratitude and cherish every moment, enjoy every laugh, and make every memory count. And I hope you can use this to be inspired during your own storms and see them as steppingstones to finding your greater purpose.

Tiffiny Roper

Tiffiny Roper is on a mission to create amazing female leaders of tomorrow that this world desperately needs. She accomplishes this as a Life Coach for Moms of young daughters, working passionately with them to reach their goals and becoming confident role models for their daughters. In doing so, they live with a new purpose-driven life, filled with joy, and inspire those around them to do the same, starting with their own daughters.

She uses her 20 years of Project Management experience to keep Moms accountable in hitting their goals. She's also a speaker and best-selling author that loves creating memories with her husband of over 20 years and twin daughters, including coaching their softball team and volunteering with their Girl Scout troop.

You can reach Tiffiny at tiffiny@girlmomcoaching.com or request to join her private Facebook group for Girl Moms at https://www. facebook.com/groups/girlmomcoaching.

AFTERWORD

Your Chapter Awaits

Dear Reader,

As you turn this final page, you might find yourself reflecting on the journey you've just experienced through these words. Each story you read is a tapestry of dreams, struggles, triumphs, and the relentless spirit of its creator. Now, imagine a world where your story joins these ranks – where your voice, your experiences, and your unique perspective are shared and celebrated.

This is not just an invitation; it's a call to action from Action Takers Publishing. We believe in the power of stories to transform, inspire, and connect humankind. More importantly, we believe in your story and its potential to make a significant impact on the planet.

Why wait for "someday" to tell your story? The time is now, and the world is ready to listen. Whether it's a tale of adventure, a deeply personal memoir, a groundbreaking idea, or a story that has been quietly growing in your heart, it deserves to be told.

At Action Takers Publishing, led by our Founder & CEO, Lynda Sunshine West, we specialize in turning visions into reality. We understand the journey of transforming a personal narrative into a published book – it's a journey of courage, creativity, and breaking through fears. Our team is dedicated to guiding you through every step of this exhilarating process, from the initial draft to the moment your book is held in the hands of eager readers across the globe.

Join our vibrant community of authors, a diverse group of storytellers who have dared to make their voices heard. With us, you'll find more than just a publisher; you'll discover a supportive network of mentors, editors, and fellow authors who are all committed to the success of your story.

Take the leap. Embrace the thrill of seeing your name on the cover of your very own book. Contact us at Action Takers Publishing, and let's embark on this remarkable journey together. Your story matters, and the time to share it with the world is now.

Nothing Happens Without Action.

Lynda Sunshine West

Founder of Action Takers Publishing

https://www.actiontakerspublishing.com/

p.s. Remember, every great story begins with a simple decision to start writing. Yours is no different. Let's make it happen, together.

READER BONUS!

Dear Reader,

As a thank you for your support, Action Takers Publishing would like to offer you a special reader bonus. Learn how to become an Amazon bestselling author by downloading "How to Become an Amazon Bestseller—Top Strategies Revealed."

You have a story to tell. It's time to tell it.

If you've ever thought about sharing your story and becoming an author, this ebook will give you tips for after you've published. This comprehensive ebook is designed to provide you with the tools and knowledge you need to bring your book to life and turn it into a successful venture.

Ready to become a bestselling author? Download your copy today at https://actiontakerspublishing.com/amazonbestseller. As an Action Taker, you know there's no time like the present.

BS Tips

READER BONUS!